THE OXFORD
MINI HISTORY
OF
BRITAIN

VOLUME I

THE OXFORD
MINI HISTORY OF BRITAIN

This five-volume series, edited by Kenneth O. Morgan, is the work of ten historians who are all distinguished authorities in their fields.

VOLUME I. ROMAN AND ANGLO-SAXON BRITAIN
 PETER SALWAY, The Open University. *Roman Britain*
 JOHN BLAIR, The Queen's College, Oxford. *The Anglo-Saxons*

VOLUME II. THE MIDDLE AGES
 JOHN GILLINGHAM, London School of Economics and Political Science. *The Early Middle Ages*
 RALPH A. GRIFFITHS, University College of Swansea. *The Later Middle Ages*

VOLUME III. THE TUDORS AND STUARTS
 JOHN GUY, University of Bristol. *The Tudor Age*
 JOHN MORRILL, Selwyn College, Cambridge. *The Stuarts*

VOLUME IV. THE EIGHTEENTH AND EARLY
 NINETEENTH CENTURIES
 PAUL LANGFORD, Lincoln College, Oxford. *The Eighteenth Century*
 CHRISTOPHER HARVIE, University of Tübingen. *Revolution and the Rule of Law*

VOLUME V. THE MODERN AGE
 H. C. G. MATTHEW, St Hugh's College, Oxford. *The Liberal Age*
 KENNETH O. MORGAN, University College of Wales, Aberystwyth. *The Twentieth Century*

THE OXFORD
MINI HISTORY
OF
BRITAIN

EDITED BY
KENNETH O. MORGAN

VOLUME I
ROMAN AND
ANGLO-SAXON BRITAIN

Oxford   New York
OXFORD UNIVERSITY PRESS
1989

The text of this edition first published 1984 in The Oxford Illustrated History of Britain
First issued (with revisions) as an Oxford University Press paperback 1988 in
The Oxford History of Britain
This edition produced exclusively for The Leisure Circle
by Oxford University Press and first issued 1989

Printed and bound in Great Britain by
Cox & Wyman Ltd, Reading

CONTENTS

LIST OF MAPS

THE OXFORD
MINI HISTORY
OF
BRITAIN

1. *Roman Britain*

(*c*.55 BC—*c*. AD 440)

PETER SALWAY

The Beginnings of British History

IN Roman times Britain had as many people as at its peak in the Middle Ages. For four centuries it was an integral part of a single political system that stretched from Turkey to Portugal and from the Red Sea to the Tyne and beyond. Its involvement with Rome started before the Conquest launched by Claudius in AD 43, and it continued to be a part of the Roman world for some time after the final break with Roman rule. We are dealing with a full half-millennium of the history of Britain.

The origins of later Britain go back beyond the Roman period. Aspects of the society the Romans found in Britain were beginning to emerge in the Neolithic and Early Bronze Ages. At the time of the Roman Conquest, the culture of Britain had something like fifteen hundred to two thousand years of development behind it—although the prehistorians are greatly divided on the details. By the end of the pre-Roman Iron Age, society had evolved forms of organization closely similar to those encountered by the Romans elsewhere in north-western Europe, and had adopted versions of the culture and language we loosely call 'Celtic'. Outside the imperial frontiers in Britain these continued largely unchanged; inside, the Celtic substratum persisted, assimilated and adapted by Rome in ways not in general closely paralleled by modern colonial empires.

Why, then, are we not either starting this *History of Britain* before the Romans, or consigning Roman Britain, as some modern writers would have us do, to 'prehistory'? The answer lies in the real distinction between the Roman period and what went before. There is some truth in the assertion that the study of Roman Britain is prehistory, in the sense that we have to lean very heavily on archaeology—and this is also true of the early Anglo-Saxon period. However, our sources for Britain are by no means solely archaeological, and the interpretation of the material remains themselves cannot be divorced from the study of the written sources. It is true that the quantity of contemporary or near-contemporary literary evidence is not great in comparison with later periods but there is enough to be significant. Moreover, we have the very considerable remains of the once huge routine output of a literate society—and in a form not subject to the inevitable corruptions of the Greek and Latin literary texts, which have largely survived only by being copied and re-copied by hand down the centuries. Actual examples of writing found in Britain, mostly as inscriptions on stone but some in other forms, constitute a major primary source for the Romano-British period. They include trade marks on manufactured goods; a small but growing number of personal letters and other documents in a variety of materials, discovered in excavations; even graffiti—the everyday writing and reading matter of ordinary people. Nor can we ignore the specialized and difficult but rewarding study of Roman coinage, which had a peculiarly important part in the politics and economics of the Roman world. Not only was the currency itself manipulated by government as money, but also the wording and images upon the coins were consistently exploited as a powerful medium for mass propaganda which possessed the insistence of a television commercial repeated over and over again. The ability to read was, admittedly, very much commoner in the towns than in the Romano-British countryside but it was compulsory in the army and essential in many other walks of life. It was certainly not, as in other ages, restricted to a small or specialized class.

The critical difference between Roman Britain and what went

before is that its society was literate, perhaps more literate than at any other time till the end of the Middle Ages. Alongside and allied to this is the fact that it was a world dominated by the rule of law, which closely regulated the relations between the individual and the State and between one man and another, however corruptly or inefficiently it might often have been administered. As a society that became more and more dominated by regulations and procedures contained in official documents, the contrast between Roman Britain and the country as it was at the end of the Iron Age is startling. Then, even at the top of the social scale, where the import of Roman luxury goods was a notable feature, writing was totally absent except on the splendid but limited coinage—and even on that the language employed was almost universally Latin and the moneyers themselves often Roman.

Once Julius Caesar's expeditions of 55 and 54 BC had pointed the way, it was more or less inevitable that Rome would try her hand at conquest. Romans did not acknowledge any limit on their right to expand their rule: indeed they saw it as a divine mission. From Caesar onwards, Britain occupied a particular and significant place in the Roman consciousness. The Roman period is a turning-point, not so much in the underlying story of man's settlement of the land of Britain but in the country's emergence from prehistory into history.

The character of the physical geography of a country has a great effect on how people live, and Britain is no exception. Its outstanding permanent characteristic is the broad division between 'highland' and 'lowland'—in rough terms, between the north and west of mainland Britain and the south and east—but it is a distinction which can be overdone in historical analysis. Moreover, in Britain man has shown a considerable capacity to adapt the landscape, sometimes intentionally, often in pursuit of some other end, such as fuel. There have also been important fluctuations in the physical conditions, especially in the relative level of land and sea, with considerable effects on the coastline and inland on the pattern and level of rivers. To what extent the causes were climatic or a matter of movements in the geology is uncertain. In general, such evidence as we have for the Roman period suggests that the climate was broadly similar to present-day Britain. A period of relatively high sea-level was succeeded in the first century AD by a 'marine regression', opening up new lands for exploitation. In the third century the onset of rather wetter climatic conditions seems to be revealed by evidence of flooding in many parts of Europe, with serious problems for low-lying land, rivers, and harbours. So it would seem that climatic conditions were by no means constant throughout the period.

The once popular belief that Britain was largely covered with forest until cleared by the Anglo-Saxons is now discredited. By the Roman Conquest, although there was still a great deal of natural forest, the population had already grown to something of the order it was under the Romans, two or three times greater than during the reign of William the Conqueror (1066–87). The proportion of forest to open, settled landscape had dropped to the level of the later Middle Ages. From about 1300 BC what was to become the classic Iron Age pattern had started to take shape: hill-forts, isolated farms or groups of farms sometimes amounting to villages (often surrounded by small enclosures), larger expanses of permanent fields, woodland, and great open stretches of pasture. In the last 600 years before Caesar, Britain adopted many of the characteristics of the successive phases of the Continental Iron Age, though often with insular variations. This has led to unresolved debate among the prehistorians as to whether the changes that succeeded one another primarily reflect actual invasions on a substantial scale, the arrival of relatively small numbers of influential or conquering newcomers (as later the Normans), or the exchange of ideas through travel and trade. But whatever the mechanism, Britain had reached the point by Caesar's time where, as he himself says, the tribes he met in the parts he penetrated—the south and east—were very similar to those he encountered in Gaul. Beyond these, archaeology reveals that there were some less-advanced peoples, but all of them seem to have shared the same British version of the Celtic language and a broadly similar culture.

There is some reason to think that the tribal system we find in Britain in Claudian times was not fully developed in Caesar's, and there are other important changes in the period between the Roman invasions which we shall examine later. In southern Gaul, the native tribes had largely passed from rule by kings to elective magistracies and tribal councils, but in northern Gaul kingship was still common when Caesar arrived. In Britain it was to remain so down to Claudius, though there are some signs of joint or divided rule by pairs of kings. Society divided broadly into a warrior aristocracy and a largely agricultural commons. The priests, the druids, were a third group whose position and function is debated, though for Britain at least the evidence is against the popular notion of their having a prominent political role. The Celts were characterized by quarrelsomeness, both within the tribe and in their indulgence in inter-tribal warfare. Only on rare occasions, in the face of great danger, would Celtic tribes combine to choose a single leader; though in Gaul at least there was some tradition of periodic gatherings of prominent men from various tribes. There was little or no 'national' sentiment.

By Caesar's day, close relationships had been established between southern Britain and northern Gaul. The pattern of archaeological finds reveals two main groups of routes by which goods and people travelled between the countries. The most important at this time was between Brittany and Lower Normandy (in ancient times known collectively as Armorica) and south-west Britain, particularly through a port at Hengistbury Head in Dorset. The other routes were from Upper Normandy and the Low Countries, the lands between the mouths of the Seine and Rhine, to southern and eastern England. Caesar moreover reports that 'within living memory' a Gallic ruler had exercised power in Britain as well as his own homeland, and he was not only to find British contingents fighting alongside his Gallic enemies but to be thwarted by fugitives seeking refuge from Rome with friends or kin across the Channel.

To understand why Caesar was in Gaul and what may have prompted his campaigns in Britain we need to look briefly at the condition of Rome at this time. Rome's expansion in the third and second centuries BC from being an Italian city state to the greatest power in the Mediterranean had been under her traditional form of government. This was theoretically democratic, with assemblies of the people and annually elected magistrates, but in practice public office was held century after century by a relatively small number of aristocratic families. The senate, notionally an advisory body, came to have a dominant role, being composed of magistrates and all those who had previously been elected to the qualifying magistracies. The highest offices, the two annual consulships, were almost exclusively held by an even smaller group within the senatorial class, and its families possessed special prestige. Religious and social attitudes, closely intertwined, placed a very high value on veneration of the family ancestors and the preservation of family honour. It was a characteristic of the classical world that a man's reputation—what his peers thought of him—was of the highest importance. At Rome, the individual aristocrat was under constant pressure, both of family duty and personal ambition, to emulate his forebears by pursuing a public career and by striving for the highest office.

Reputation was won by success primarily in two fields—the law and the army. A senatorial career normally included posts in each area. Of the two, proven military prowess won the greater prestige. Holding certain senior offices, even below the consulship, brought with it eligibility to command armies and govern provinces abroad. Caesar's contemporary, the orator, politician, and moralist Cicero, states categorically what conferred the greatest personal status: there was more glory to be won by extending the empire than by administering it.

In the ancient world, wars of conquest usually showed a

handsome profit for the victor. The immense wealth brought into Rome by her conquests and the opportunities and temptations offered by her Mediterranean empire put intolerable strains on the political and social system that had been adequate for a small Italian state. By the middle of the first century BC, the Roman Republic was falling apart. The old conventions within the governing class could not cope. Ambition to join the select few at the top had been replaced by an inability to tolerate even equals in power and fame.

Part of the visible prestige of a great Roman aristocrat had long been the number of people dependent upon him. Indeed whole communities could regard themselves as among his 'clients'. Such 'patronage' was a feature of society that was to be of great importance to provinces such as Britain, otherwise far from the centre of power. By the first century BC, the old citizen armies, raised for a specific war, had been replaced by professionals. The senate made the fatal mistake of allowing these new soldiers to become dependent upon their own generals rather than the State for the rewards of service, particularly the all-important provision on retirement. The conditions for recurrent civil war were now all present and the Republic effectively doomed. Attitudes, practices, and social relationships had been set up that were to haunt Rome for the rest of her history. For Britain, it was not only the great events of the subsequent history of the empire that directly affected her destiny, but also the extraordinary success the Romans had in transmitting their values to the populations they absorbed— particularly to the native ruling classes. Indeed, the creation of a common upper-class culture, critical to the successful working of the empire itself, was in many ways also central in its downfall. The story of Britain in Roman times reflects this fundamental pattern.

Julius Caesar's conquest of Gaul must be looked at in the context of the struggle for power in the closing years of the Republic. We shall probably never know exactly why he launched his two expeditions to Britain in 55 and 54 BC nor whether he intended conquest—though there is a possible parallel in his punitive foray across the Rhine into Germany. More important were the consequences for the future. In immediate military terms the results were modest, though we do not hear of Britons fighting in Gaul again. Because of the explosive state of Gaul, Caesar was prevented from following up his victories and from taking advantage of the surrender of the temporary confederation of the British tribes. Indeed, a Roman historian writing in the next century even represented a British leader as claiming the 'repulse' of Caesar by the ancestors of his hearers.

Caesar's British enterprise made a lasting impression on Rome, however. Britain was a remote, almost fabled island across the 'Ocean', a fearsome sea to Romans as yet unaccustomed· to the tidal conditions outside the Mediterranean. Britain was beyond the known world. In two brief campaigns Caesar had put Britain on the Roman map. Retaining its aura of mystery, it would henceforth always occupy an alluring place in the minds of those eager for military ambition—and Caesar had set a goal and a precedent for subsequent members of the Julian family. Moreover his experiences—he had a number of close shaves at the hands not only of the British but also of the elements—provided practical lessons for a future expeditionary commander.

Caesar had also set important precedents for intervention in Britain. He had received the surrender of powerful kings and accepted the friendship of others. A tribute—or annual tax—to be paid to Rome had been imposed. He had also installed as king of the Trinovantes of Essex a young prince who had fled to him in Gaul. The father of this prince had been killed by Cassivellaunus, the same Briton who was elected by the British confederation to lead them against Caesar—and who was now forbidden to interfere with the Trinovantes. Rome could, therefore, claim some sort of overlordship, the right to exact payments and an obligation to protect her friends, if she chose to move. (Rome rarely did so in fact, unless it was in her own interest: many small countries under her nominal protection failed to appreciate this basic fact of ancient life, with unfortunate consequences.) But precedent, we may remember, was important to the Romans, and after Caesar they had ample.

For two decades after Caesar, the attention of the Roman world was monopolized by the series of civil wars that brought the Republic to an end and put Caesar's adopted heir Octavian (later to assume the name Augustus) into power. Caesar had himself taken no action when his erstwhile Gallic friend Commius, whom he had installed as king of the Atrebates in Gaul, joined the great revolt. The crushing of that revolt saw Commius in flight to Britain—where he had earlier been used as Caesar's agent—to found a dynasty among the British Atrebates. The lack of Roman interest in Britain at this time is understandable. More interesting for us is that we are now beginning to identify tribes and plot the history of dynasties. Commius' own case is particularly intriguing. His rule over a Roman-devised 'client' kingdom of Gallic Atrebates and the Morini of the Channel coast north of the Seine had put him in control of much of the area through which the routes from the main concentration of 'Belgae', straddling the Meuse, ran towards Britain. Somewhat earlier than Caesar, there seems to have been the beginning of a movement from the Belgic part of Gaul into Britain which probably accelerated as Caesar's conquests progressed, establishing, at the least, related royal houses in Britain.

In the course of the first century BC, Belgic culture became dominant in southern Britain, even among tribes themselves not Belgic. The pattern of life was changing. The division of labour in society became more pronounced, with more and more activities, such as pottery-making, becoming the preserve of craftsmen rather than domestic. British art reached a magnificent peak, especially in metalwork, all swirling motifs and fine enamelling, but it concentrated on the equipping of warrior chiefs and possibly the adornment of shrines. In the most Belgicized areas, hill-forts tended to give way to large settlements on lower ground, sometimes with their approaches defended by great running earthworks. These have been seen as the forerunners of Roman towns, though some were more in the nature of royal residences than urban in the contemporary Mediterranean sense. But for the future of the British landscape the most interesting change is the widespread emergence, particularly in the period between Caesar and Claudius (54 BC–AD 43), of a more permanent pattern of rural land settlement, with regular boundaries that suggest regular tenure. There is a growing feeling among archaeologists that this period may mark the beginning of a framework of land-division that has persisted to the present day. Those who worked and owned the land have certainly changed many times. The skeleton of the landscape, in this credible hypothesis, has survived into modern times.

In the year before his first expedition Caesar had fought and destroyed at sea the fleet of the Veneti of Brittany, whose ships had controlled the carrying trade between Armorica and south-west Britain. About this time, archaeology shows a dramatic switch in emphasis to the routes between Belgic Gaul and the south and east of Britain. Henceforth, the sea passages from the Seine to the Southampton area, the short crossings from Boulogne to Kent, and the route from the Rhine and the Low Countries to the estuaries of Essex were paramount. It is not, perhaps, surprising to find that the greatest wealth and sophistication were now in these areas of Britain. From 12 BC, indeed, when Augustus launched his armies on the conquest of Holland and Germany, the new importance of the northern links with Britain must have further sharply increased. Although in the long run Augustus' attempt to extend the empire to the Elbe failed, from this time large Roman armies were permanently on the Rhine. Britain was exporting corn, hides, cattle, and iron to the empire, all items of vital importance to the Roman military effort. Recent research has indicated that the technologically efficient British agriculture was producing, at least in grain, a large surplus over the subsistence needs of its people. We may reasonably surmise that the increasing wealth, the changes in society, and even the new pattern of British agriculture were stimulated, perhaps even caused, by the opportunities offered by the needs of the army of the Rhine and the emerging civil markets of the new Roman provinces across the Channel.

In his early days Augustus was acutely conscious of the legacy of Caesar's memory and the urgent need to establish a military reputation for himself. Even before his final defeat of Mark Antony he seems to have planned an invasion of Britain; and at least two more attempts were made to put it into effect. All were frustrated by more pressing demands. After 26 BC, however, he was content to let the imminent conquest of Britain remain an uncorrected impression that served as useful propaganda at Rome, while developing diplomatic relations that may have sprung out of negotiations we know were already in progress, perhaps to re-establish Caesar's taxation. Strabo, an author writing late in Augustus' reign or under his successor Tiberius, confirms that the Britons were paying heavy customs dues to Rome on their import and export trade. He seems to reflect a party line that sought to justify the shift in policy away from invasion when he claims that Rome forbore to make the easy conquest of Britain because taxation without occupation was more profitable. The Britons, he adds significantly, posed no military threat.

Commius was succeeded on his British throne by a son, Tincommius, and around 15 BC there seems to have been a reversal of attitude which put this important kingdom at the British end of the Seine-Southampton route into friendship with Rome. The reason may have been the growing power of one British tribe, the Catuvellauni, centred in Hertfordshire. Whether they had recently coalesced from smaller clans or had already been the force behind Cassivellaunus is uncertain; but the history of Britain up to the Claudian conquest is now dominated by Catuvellaunian expansion. For the time being, however, Rome chose to turn a blind eye. Even the expulsion of Tincommius and another British king, and their seeking refuge with Augustus, were only treated by Rome as support for the Augustan claim to exercise virtual sway over Britain, propaganda for internal consumption. Indeed, there is every sign the Catuvellauni were careful not to display open hostility. The balance was mutually profitable to the governing classes on both sides. British aristocrats were enjoying the imports from the empire, while the list of exports that the Roman author thinks worthy of mention shows that the Britons were not only paying for these luxuries with supplies important to the army: by ending gold, silver, slaves, and hunting dogs they had also become a source of commodities of direct interest to the emperor himself and to the rich at Rome. After disaster in Germany in AD 9, Augustus and his successor Tiberius erected non-intervention outside the empire into a principle—the absolute opposite of previous Augustan practice. It must, however, be a measure of the satisfactory nature of the working relationship that Cunobelinus, Shakespeare's Cymbeline, now king of the Catuvellauni, managed to avoid Roman retribution even when he took over the territory of Caesar's old protégés, the Trinovantes, and transferred the centre of his kingdom to Colchester. He now had command of the lucrative route to the Rhine. Within Britain he could cut the supply of their status symbols to other British princes at will; and whether by conquest or other means the power and influence of his kingdom continued to expand.

The Roman Conquest

The state of mutual toleration, satisfactory as it doubtless was for Rome and the Catuvellauni—but perhaps not so welcome to other Britons—started to crumble when the unstable Gaius (Caligula) succeeded Tiberius. At some point in this period, Cunobelinus expelled one of his sons, who eventually fled to the emperor, to whom he made a formal act of submission. Gaius not only claimed the surrender of Britain; he also gave orders for an invasion. These he subsequently countermanded, but only at the last minute, and it is this that is important. The staff work had been done, the whole massive process of build-up to an invasion had been gone through, not as manœuvres but as a real operation, and the Roman public had been reminded of unfinished business. Everything lay ready for a more determined hand.

The murder of Gaius hoisted unceremoniously to the throne his uncle Claudius, previously ignored by the rest of the imperial family under the mistaken notion that he was of defective intelligence. In fact, he combined common sense, an original mind bordering on the eccentric, a professional interest in history, and a profound veneration for Roman tradition. Faced soon after his elevation by a serious military revolt, the need to establish his reputation with the troops and gain respect at Rome must have been obvious to him. Such a man could hardly miss the chance of military glory offered by Britain and the opportunity not only to carry out the invasion cancelled by Augustus and Gaius before him but even to outdo Julius Caesar himself. Personal and family reputation could not be better served.

There was a pretext, too—and one which could be referred back to sound precedent and provided a strategic reason for intervention. Cunobelinus was now dead, and his realm had fallen into the hands of two other aggressive sons—Caratacus and Togodumnus. The eastern entrance to Britain was, therefore, unreliable. In the south, pressure on Tincommius' old kingdom had reduced it to a rump on the coast: now that entrance, too, closed when an internal coup expelled Tincommius' brother, Verica. The latter, in the time-honoured fashion, also fled to the emperor. All Britain seemed to be turning hostile, and the valuable traffic between it and the empire was threatened. Like Caesar, Claudius could respond to an appeal from a British prince.

Caesar had relied upon inspired generalship and the devotion of the troops who had served long under him. The new standing regular army that Augustus and his successors had created still depended on generalship, but was more firmly based on meticulous organization and training and the permanence of its institutions. At this period, the legions, the backbone of the army, recruited only from Roman citizens, still drew most of their men from Italy. Gradually, the citizen colonies founded in the older provinces outside Italy were to provide men for the military career. Each legion had an establishment of something over five thousand men, mostly heavy infantry, backed by small cavalry contingents, catapults, and other engines of war. The legions also provided a wide range of skilled craftsmen and administrators; and individual soldiers, all of whom were required to read and write, could be used on a vast range of government tasks. The 'auxiliary' units were, in the first half of the first century AD, evolving from native irregulars under their own chieftains into regular regiments of provincials, mostly non-citizen, but with Roman commanders. These regiments were normally five hundred strong, cavalry, infantry, or mixed, with status and pay inferior to those of the legions. Both legionaries and auxiliaries, however, enjoyed those extreme rarities in the ancient world, a regular money wage, an assured career, and provision for retirement. Education, training, and opportunities for self-advancement—not to mention self-enrichment—made the army a major force in social mobility. Both serving and retired soldiers were persons of consequence in their communities. Auxiliaries automatically received Roman citizenship on retirement and their sons were eligible to join the legions. These units thus provided a continuous process of turning unlettered barbarians into literate Roman citizens and were a major element in the assimilation of new peoples into the empire.

The force assembled to sail to Britain in AD 43 comprised four legions and about the same number of auxiliary troops, around 40,000 men in all. Facing this disciplined machine, the British forces retained their old character. The permanent warriors were the aristocracy; their favourite weapon was the chariot, which they used for rapid transport in and out of battle and in the handling of which their drivers were extremely skilled. The exact status of the cavalry is uncertain: they were probably men who could provide their own horses, but it is not clear that their prime occupation in life was fighting. The mass of the British armies was the levies, summoned from the farms. Unlike the armoured Romans, the Britons wore little or no body protection and depended on speed, impetus, and the long slashing sword. Before they could get near to Romans in battle order they were liable to lose many men to the clouds of Roman javelins; and in hand-to-hand combat their long blades were at a disadvantage faced with the closed ranks and short stabbing swords of the enemy infantry. Successes by these Celtic troops against the Romans were usually gained in surprise attacks, in ambushes, and when overwhelming detached units by sheer numbers. They could rarely match the legions in pitched battle, and Roman commanders aimed to force them out into the open or to pen them behind ramparts where Roman siegecraft and artillery could beat them down or starve them out. But perhaps their greatest disadvantage in the face of the Romans was that as farmer-soldiers they could only stay in the field for a short part of the year. If they were not sent home, the population starved. The supply system of the Roman army, on the contrary, permitted it to campaign as long as the weather permitted, and to build fortified, well-stocked camps in which to sit out each winter. Such a system permitted a war to be carried on for year after year, and provided the basis for the garrisoning required for permanent occupation. Faced with such an opponent, it is remarkable that the British resisted so long and so hard.

The invasion met with fierce resistance from some of the British tribes. Others, no doubt not sorry to see the Catuvellaunian hegemony in southern Britain destroyed, surrendered easily or joined the Romans. The campaign was crowned by the submission of eleven British kings to the emperor and his triumphant entry into Colchester, for which he had joined his advancing forces, complete with elephants. His delight was marked by the revival of ancient rituals once performed by Republican victors and the proud proclamation of the extension of empire, in which the Conquest of Ocean once more figured large (it was no hollow boast: the army had at first refused to sail).

By AD 47 the Claudian armies occupied Britain as far as the Severn and the Trent. The work of organizing Britain as a regular province was now in progress. Its governorship enjoyed high status. It was reserved for ex-consuls and carried with it the command of an exceptionally large group of legions. In its first century and a half as a province, men of particular distinction were regularly chosen. It was not only a military challenge where reputations could be won, but—though we shall never have the figures to compare income from Britain with expenditure on its defence and administration—it was regarded as a land of natural abundance as late as the fourth century. By AD 47, indeed, the exploitation of Britain's mineral resources—one of the chief objectives of victory—had begun (the silver-bearing lead of the Mendips was being mined under state control by this date). It might have saved Rome much trouble and expense if she had limited her conquest to the area she already controlled; but it is very doubtful whether Roman ambition could long have been restrained, even if the warlike and unstable tribes of the north and Wales had not been a threat to the peaceful development of the south. As it was, the events of the next two or three years committed Rome to a different course.

Roman practice in the provinces was always to shift as much of the burden of administration on to loyal locals as soon as might be. The Claudian intention seems to have been to employ 'client' kings as far as possible—the most economical method, where they were reliable. A substantial part of the south, including Verica's old kingdom, was put in the hands of one Cogidubnus, who may not have been a native Briton. The Iceni of Norfolk were kept as 'allies'; and an understanding was reached beyond the border of Roman rule with Cartimandua, queen of the Brigantes (a vast grouping of clans that encompassed most of northern England), with the object of securing the province from attack from the north. One success of this policy was when Cartimandua handed over the fugitive Caratacus to Claudius; another was the enduring loyalty of Cogidubnus, which was almost certainly of critical importance during later crises in Britain.

The rest of the province the governor would expect to administer chiefly through the tribes, reorganized as Roman local government units (*civitates*) with their nobles formed into councils and holding local magistracies—scaled-down versions of the Roman constitution, in fact, but often adapting existing institutions. In addition, throughout the province ran the writ of the chief financial secretary of Britain, the *procurator provinciae*. These provincial procurators reported direct to the emperor. This was natural enough, since they had particular responsibilities for crown land (the emperors automatically acquired the royal estates of defeated enemies, besides much else by inheritance or confiscation) and crown monopolies; but they also acted as a check on the governor, the emperor's military and judicial representative. Friction was not uncommon and not wholly unintentional.

The train of events that made it certain the province would not remain confined to the south started in AD 47 with the Roman response to raids from outside. Measures taken included not only counter-attacks but also the disarming of Britons within the province. This was bound to have come eventually, since civilians were forbidden to carry arms within the empire except in certain very limited circumstances— something that says much about everyday security in Roman times—but those who had voluntarily submitted to Rome had not expected it to apply to them. The Iceni revolted and were put down by force: the true status of the client kingdoms had now been made plain. The next step was the moving forward of the legion that had been stationed at Colchester and its replacement in AD 49 by a colony of Roman legionary veterans. This was intended as the seat of the Imperial Cult—the formal worship of Rome and the Imperial Family which focused the loyalty of the province—and the veterans were to act as a bulwark against possible revolt. In practice, Colchester was now an ungarrisoned civil city. Perhaps at the same moment, London was founded as a supply port. It is possible that from its beginning it was intended in due course to become the administrative centre of Britain as well. It was in all probability created as a deliberate act, rather than emerging out of a casual settlement of traders, as was formerly thought. The pre-eminence of the Essex coast was now challenged by the Thames, and London's position at the hub of the radiating system of main roads now being built, designed for official purposes, very soon made it also the business centre of the province.

The 50s were a decade of urban development. Only the agricultural hinterland remained largely unchanged, at least on the surface, and progress towards the universal adoption of the money economy was slow. By AD 60, however, with the governor, Suetonius Paullinus, about to subdue the troublesome tribes of North Wales, the province looked set to progress steadily. What went wrong? Why did the provincials, led by Rome's old friends the Iceni and Trinovantes, turn into a raging horde, set on destroying every trace of Rome?

We have only the Roman account, but it is enough to reveal maladministration ranging from the callously negligent to the undeniably criminal. Tacitus makes a general comment on the British character: 'The Britons bear conscription, the tribute and their other obligations to the empire without complaint, provided there is no injustice. That they take extremely ill; for they can bear to be ruled by others but not to be their slaves.' The responsibility for AD 61 cannot be confined to the procurator alone, the traditional villain of the piece. The governor has to take a share, and it cannot stop there. The young Nero, now on the throne, can hardly be blamed directly, for he was under the influence of his 'good' advisers, Burrus, the praetorian prefect, and the philosopher and dramatist Seneca. Of these two, it seems very likely that Seneca, at least, knew what was going on in Britain because he suddenly recalled, in a ruthless manner, large sums of money he had been lending to leading Britons at a high rate of interest. Reports coming out of Britain may well have indicated unrest that might put his investment at risk. In the event, the action fuelled the flames. There are two main threads to the grievances, represented respectively by the Iceni and the Trinovantes. At his death, Boudica's husband, Prasutagus, the client king of the Iceni, had left half his possessions to the emperor, expecting that this would protect his kingdom and family. Agents of the procurator and of the governor, however, had treated this as if it were the unconditional surrender of an enemy. The king's property was confiscated, nobles were expelled from their estates, and taxation and conscription enforced. The Trinovantes were suffering other insults. The main burden of the Imperial Cult, designed to promote loyalty to the emperor, had fallen on their nobles, while the Roman colonists—significantly with the encouragement of serving soldiers—seized their lands and treated them with contempt. They (and probably the aristocracies of other *civitates*) were facing financial ruin, the last straw being the reclaiming of grants made by Claudius and the recall of Seneca's loans. The Imperial Cult, as represented by the Temple of the Deified Claudius at Colchester, was, ironically, the focus of British hatred.

In answer to Boudica's protests, she was flogged and her daughters raped. Rousing her own tribe and her Trinovantian neighbours and carrying other *civitates* with her (but clearly not Cogidubnus) she swept through southern Britain, burning Colchester, London, and Verulamium (near St. Albans), torturing every Roman or Roman sympathizer she could catch, and inflicting devastating defeats on the few Roman units that had been left in that part of the country. The governor only just avoided the total loss of the province. After the eventual victory when he had brought her to battle his retribution was all the more extreme. For a while it looked as if the ruin of the province of Britain would now ironically be achieved at Roman hands. Nero, indeed, at one stage in his reign—possibly earlier, perhaps now—had been inclined to abandon Britain altogether.

In the end two factors saved the province: the intervention of a remarkable new provincial procurator, Classicianus, himself of Gallic origin, and the recall to Rome of the governor.

The recovery that occupied Britain for the decade after Boudica was genuine but unspectacular. There is some evidence that under the last governor appointed by Nero it was beginning to accelerate. But the outbreak of civil war across the empire in AD 69 ('The Year of the Four Emperors') revived the spectre of generals fighting for supremacy. However, the outcome of the wars brought in a vigorous new administration in the persons of the Flavian emperors. For Britain, this spelled provincial renewal and the expansion of Roman power. As Tacitus says, 'Now come great generals and magnificent armies, and with them the hopes of our enemies fall into ruin.'

While the Roman world had been distracted by the civil wars, a fresh outbreak of strife among the Brigantes had lost Cartimandua her kingdom and embroiled the Roman army. The north of Britain was no longer secure. The old policy of client kingship, already shaken by Boudica and previous Brigantian disturbances, was finally discredited. Within a few years even Cogidubnus was probably pensioned off to live in the splendid villa of Fishbourne. By AD 84 or 84 a succession of first-rate governors had carried Roman arms to the far north of Scotland and garrisons to the edge of the Highlands—and were pressing ahead with Romanization. Tacitus, in describing the work of his father-in-law Agricola, uses words that can characterize the Flavian period as a whole:

In order to encourage a truculent population that dwelled in scattered settlements (and was thus only too ready to fall to fighting) to live in a peaceful and inactive manner by offering it the pleasures that would follow on such a way of living, Agricola urged these people privately, and helped them officially, to build temples, public squares with public buildings (*fora*), and private houses (*domus*). He praised those who responded quickly, and severely criticized laggards. In this way, competition for public recognition took the place of compulsion. Moreover he had the children of the leading Britons educated in the civilized arts and openly placed the natural ability of the Britons above that of the Gauls, however well trained. The result was that those who had once shunned the Latin language now sought fluency and eloquence in it. Roman dress, too, became popular and the toga was frequently seen. Little by little there was a slide toward the allurements of degeneracy: assembly-rooms (*porticus*), bathing establishments and smart dinner parties. In their inexperience the Britons called it civilization when it was really all part of their servitude.

To a certain extent this urbanization under the Flavians was less than completely successful. The core of its more securely-based development can reasonably be associated with the visit of the Emperor Hadrian to Britain in person in 122, when existing schemes were revived or replaced and vast new works put in hand. But, looked at in longer perspective, the period from AD 70 to the 160s is the age when Britain truly became Roman and its lasting features as part of the empire emerged. Central to this absorption into the Roman system was the more or less universal devolution of the burden of routine adminis-tration to the local aristocracies that replaced the client king-doms. It was crucially important to this policy to win over the native aristocracy whose confidence had been so disastrously lost in the reign of Nero, and it is in this context that Tacitus must be read.

Archaeologically, we can observe in the late first century and the beginning and middle of the second century the develop-ment of the cities and towns of Roman Britain to their full extent. The administrative centres of the *civitates* were provided with civic centres: the forum and basilica that provided market, law courts, civic offices, and council chambers; the public baths which in the Roman world provided the urban centre for relaxation and social life; engineered water supplies; public monuments honouring imperial figures and local worthies; and, in a number of cases, theatres or amphitheatres. This archaeological evidence is all the more significant in that in the empire it was normally the local notables themselves (in council or as individuals) who paid for such amenities, not State or emperor. Occasionally, a great private patron with local connections might favour the town with a benefaction or by acting as friend at court. Only in rare and well-publicized instances did emperors take a part, directly or through their representatives.

The urban expansion could not, of course, have rested solely on the basis of a relatively small native aristocracy taught to accept Roman ways. Indeed, the fact that this spread of town life was followed by the appearance of many 'villas' in the countryside—at this stage mainly modest but comfortable Roman houses, often replacing native homesteads—indicates that the British gentry retained their connections with the land. Most probably they were still chiefly resident on their estates, and many ordinary farmers shared their prosperity. In this period, too, veterans discharged from the legions were principally concentrated in the small number of cities deliberately founded to take them: Colchester, Lincoln, and Gloucester. The flourishing of the towns as a whole, therefore, depended equally on the emergence, well attested, of a lively urban population made up of officials, the professions, traders, and skilled artisans.

Some of these people, particularly among the craftsmen and traders, were immigrants or visitors from other parts of the empire, and many officials were on short-term postings to the province. Nevertheless, the population of Roman Britain remained overwhelmingly Celtic. The ranks of the Roman army, too, were increasingly recruited from the provinces in which units were stationed; gradually Britons who had been, like the mass of their fellows, without the distinctive Roman citizenship when they joined the army, must, as discharged veterans with their grants of citizenship and substantial gratuities, have formed an important part of the solid centre of the Romanized society now emerging. In the towns, slaves were set up in business by their masters; and the frequent use in the Roman world of the power to set slaves free or allow them to purchase their liberty expanded the skilled labour force and added to the body of businessmen. Whatever the condition of the agricultural labourer, social mobility was high in the skilled and educated portion of society. Whilst the vast bulk of the ordinary people of Britain undoubtedly remained on the land—and we have to recall that industry too, was largely concentrated in the countryside—the towns of the Early Empire came to provide centres of public life, exchange and services for the rural hinterland, and wide opportunities of advancement at different levels of society.

Hadrian's revival of flagging Flavian initiatives was thus of major importance. But his impact on the province was great in other ways. A man of restless and extraordinary character and energy, much of his reign was taken up with tours of the provinces. One of the few emperors deliberately to set himself against the tradition of expansion of the empire, he was personally unpopular with the Roman aristocracy and many of his vast enterprises were only partially successful, though whether due to internal opposition or to flaws in planning is not always clear. In Britain there are at least three major examples. Hadrian's Wall was constructed on the line to which Roman forces had been withdrawn in stages over the thirty years since the extreme point of expansion, partly because of demands for troops elsewhere, partly due to fairly serious local reverses in the field. Such a policy suited Hadrian's general inclination to limit the empire, and the design of the Wall was brilliantly original. Partly because of this, however, detailed study of its early history has revealed a remarkable series of changes of plan within Hadrian's reign; and it must have cost many times the original estimates of the expenditure and time required for completion. Similarly, the agricultural colonization of the Fenlands of East Anglia involved water engineering on a grand scale, yet many of the farms failed after only a few years. Hadrianic London, too, saw the demolition of the substantial Flavian forum and basilica and their replacement with a complex twice the normal size. In Gaul and elsewhere Hadrian intervened to help cities erect public buildings. In London this was probably related to the presence of the emperor himself during his visit to Britain in AD 122, which is supported by the erection of a permanent fort in the city at about this time—something almost unparalleled in the cities of the empire outside Rome. But when a great fire had swept through London later in Hadrian's reign the effort to reconstruct areas that had been devastated was relatively short-lived, and in the later years of the second century London shows signs of advanced urban decay.

Hadrian's frontier line from Tyne to Solway Firth represents broadly the limit within which the province settled for most of its history. Yet there were at least three major wars of conquest northwards subsequent to Hadrian, two of them commanded in person by emperors; and for long periods garrisons were maintained at points beyond the Hadrianic line and a degree of control exercised. Indeed, within months of his death in 138 plans were in hand to launch a new invasion of Scotland; and by AD 142 the armies of his generally unmilitary successor, Antoninus Pius, had, like those of Claudius, provided him with a conquest in the prestigious field of Britain. Scotland as far as the Firth of Tay was in Roman hands, and work commenced on a new, shorter, and more simply-built linear barrier to run from the Forth to the Clyde. Elaborate commemorative stone relief sculptures, set at positions along what we know as the Antonine Wall, record the confident mood of what was to be the last period of unconstrained expansion of Roman rule.

In this early Antonine period, the developments we have seen in town and country reached their first peak. Elsewhere, the empire is generally considered to have been enjoying a golden age of tranquillity and prosperity. In Britain the economic system of the Early Empire had been fully accepted, based on a money economy and large-scale, long-distance trade. Culturally, Roman fashions were dominant, and classical art and decoration widely adopted. Perhaps, historically, the most important artistic impact on the Britons of Roman conquest was the introduction of figurative styles, particularly in sculp-

Legend:
- ⊙ Provincial capital
- ■ Legionary fortresses
- ● Coloniae
- Municipia and civitas centres
  - ◆ certain ◇ uncertain

0   50   100 miles
0 50 100 150 km

CALEDONIAN TRIBES

Antonine Wall

DUMNONII

VOTADINI

SELGOVAE

NOVANTAE

Hadrian's Wall

Carlisle   LOPOCARES   Corbridge
            TEXTOVERDI

CARVETII

BRIGANTES

GABRANTOVICES
◇ Malton

Aldborough   ■ York   PARISI
              ◇ Brough-on-Humber

SETANTII

DECEANGLI   ■ Chester

ORDOVICES   CORNOVII

Wroxeter   ● Lincoln

CORITANI   ICENI

◆ Leicester   Caistor by Norwich

CATUVELLAUNI

DEMETAE

◆ Carmarthen   SILURES   Gloucester   Verulamium   TRINOVANTES
                          DOBUNNI   ◆ Colchester
            Caerleon ■ Caerwent   Cirencester
                                                London
                          ATREBATES   ◉   CANTIACI
            BELGAE   Silchester
                      ◆ Winchester   ◆ Canterbury
DUROTRIGES   REGINI
◆ Exeter   Dorchester   ◆ Chichester

DUMNONII

SECOND-CENTURY BRITAIN

ture, wall-painting, and mosaic but also in a vast range of minor arts and crafts—jewellery, pottery, furniture, and household goods of every description. First-rate works of art from Roman Britain are relatively few compared with, say, southern Gaul, but they do exist. The middle range of material is, however, quite plentiful and it is abundantly clear that mass-produced articles were freely available. It is these, rather than the few works of high art that have survived, that reveal an everyday revolution in the way of life since the pre-Roman Iron Age. Roman pottery alone reveals the existence of a 'throw-away society' that is quite different from what went before or came after.

Because it affected the deepest levels of consciousness, the most telling evidence for the assimilation of Roman and native comes from religion. Roman Britain was a religious kaleido-scope, ranging from the formal rites of the Roman State—Jupiter, Juno, and Minerva, in particular—and the Imperial Cult that had more recently been grafted on to it, through a wide range of religions imported both from the neighbouring West and from the East, to the local Celtic cults. People from overseas often retained their own favourite practices: Diodora, a Greek priestess, dedicated an altar at Corbridge in her own language to the demi-god Heracles of Tyre; soldiers from the Netherlands set up others at Housesteads on Hadrian's Wall to their native goddesses the Alaisiagae, Baudihillia and Friagabis, Beda and Fimmilena. But for our purpose the most significant are the 'conflations' or amalgamations of classical and Celtic deities. This was a difficult and uncertain process, since Celtic religion identified its deities much less clearly than Roman, but it was very widespread. That its acceptance was more than superficial is clear, for example, from an altar in the great complex of temple and baths at Bath erected to Sulis Minerva—the native healing spirit of the hot springs conflated with the Roman goddess of wisdom—by Lucius Marcius Memor, *harus-pex*. The function of the *haruspices* was divination of the future from the entrails of sacrificial animals. This ancient practice, held in the highest honour, went back to very early Etruscan strands in Italian religion, yet it is here related to a half-Celtic deity. Again, on Hayling Island, a major shrine of the pre-Roman Iron Age—more than likely associated with the kingship of Verica—was rebuilt subsequently in Roman materials, probably by an architect from Roman Gaul commissioned by Cogidubnus. It is a particularly fine example of a very large class of distinctive shrines known to archaeologists as 'Romano-Celtic temples', found right across Britain, Gaul, and Roman Germany, and quite clearly the expression in Roman architectural terms of a pre-existing type peculiar to the Celtic peoples. They are instantly recognizable, being square, circular, or polygonal structures, usually box-like with a concentric 'ambulatory', and often set within enclosed precincts which may sometimes have preserved sacred groves from pre-Roman times.

At a much less formal level we find in Weardale a cavalry officer giving thanks to Silvanus (a Celtic rural god in Roman guise) for 'a remarkably fine boar no one had previously been able to catch', or at Greta Bridge two ladies setting up an altar to the local nymph. These are typical of the deep belief of both Celts and Romans that every place had its own deity. Romans found no difficulty in accepting these deities of place in the lands they conquered. Indeed, they showed real anxiety to find out their names and honour them, as a precaution if nothing else. The darker side was a belief in ghosts and the need to placate them. Here we are at the heart of Roman religion, very congenial to the Britons, the animistic belief in the localized spirits of hearth, home, family, and ancestors, and of places and objects outside, which long pre-dated the public adoption of the classical gods of Olympus. The black element is represented archaeologically by written curses, some still sickening to read. From Clothall near Baldock comes a lead plate bearing a message written backwards (a practice common in magic), declaring that 'Tacita is hereby cursed, and this curse shall reveal her to be putrefying like rotting blood'. It is surely not just chance that excavation of a temple at Uley in Gloucester-shire has approximately doubled the total of curse-bearing tablets known from the entire Roman world. The Britons, we are told by a classical source, were obsessed with ritual. The specifically Roman contributions were to provide new artistic and architectural forms to express religious feelings, and written language in which to make those sentiments clear and permanent. Roman religious practice, with that same sense that informed Roman law, depended on the exact performance of every act and word. The care with which the Romano-Briton phrased his dedications and curses demonstrates how well the new capacity to set wording down indelibly accorded with his own ritual inclinations.

After the invasion of Scotland, Antoninus Pius waged no more aggressive wars anywhere in the Roman world, and in the 160s the mood began to change. In Britain something had gone seriously wrong around 158. There is some evidence that the Brigantes had to be suppressed, a situation perhaps made possible by premature thinning out of troops on the ground in the Pennines under the demands of the occupation of southern Scotland; and it seems the Antonine Wall itself was temporarily lost. A brief reoccupation of Scotland, perhaps after a punitive campaign (though the chronology of this period in the north is exceptionally obscure) was followed by a definitive return to the Hadrianic line. In the reign of the next emperor, Marcus Aurelius, barbarian pressure on the frontiers of the empire generally became serious. The initiative, though Rome did not recognize it for centuries, had passed from her.

For a traveller arriving from the Continent, there was one particularly striking fashion in which Britain would have seemed different from northern Gaul, whose development it had in so many ways paralleled, allowing for the century less of time it had been under Roman rule. The permanent military presence will have made him aware that a primary concern of governors in Britain was always one of defence: there were three legions, two in the west in fortresses at Chester and at

Caerleon in South Wales, and one in the north at York, together with a very large number of auxiliary units, many occupied in containing the nominally pacified tribesmen of the hills inside the province by means of a network of forts and patrolled roads. But the most visible difference in the south was the presence of *town walls*. The building of these walls was not (other than at one period) a general response to a particular crisis. It was a leisurely process, starting in the first century with towns such as Winchester and Verulamium and still in progress in the 270s. By the early second century the three prestigious colonies had walls; and an element of civic rivalry may have stirred elsewhere. The main reason for their walls, however, had to be something sufficiently important to overcome the reluctance of Roman emperors to allow the construction of fortifications that might be held by an enemy or insurgents (locals paid for the walls, but the emperor's express permission was required); and permanent enough for the process to continue even though Britain was several times implicated in major challenges to authority. Lack of defences to the villas rules out a disorderly countryside or fear of peasant revolt. The reason must be the same factor that kept the legions in the province and the auxiliary units stationed where they were—apprehension of barbarian incursion from outside and risings in the hills within the province. The cities and towns, lying on the main roads, were the obvious targets for tribes or war parties on the move. In the ancient world city walls were more or less impregnable, except to armies with sophisticated siege machinery and the logistic support necessary to sustain a prolonged siege, or where the attackers had friends within the town. Against tribesmen, therefore, walls were a first-rate form of civic defence; and their prevalence in Britain must indicate a much greater awareness of threat than was abroad in Gaul.

The walls, however, took a long time to build, and a speedier remedy was sometimes needed. An indication of impending crisis is the appearance on a large number of urban sites in Britain of *earthwork* defences, apparently in the second half of the second century. At Cirencester, for example, an earth rampart was thrown up to link monumental stone city gates and interval towers already built, as if an urgent decision had been taken to interrupt the leisurely construction programme and put the defences into immediate commission. Of the various candidates that have been proposed for this period of crisis, the most likely seems the outbreak in the north around 180 which included barbarian penetration of the frontier, reported widespread damage, and the death of a Roman general. A much less likely context is the candidacy of a governor of Britain, Clodius Albinus, for the imperial throne in the years 193–7.

The events surrounding his attempt, however, herald a new age in the history of the empire, in the course of which Britain's fortunes diverged much more sharply from that of neighbouring Gaul. Marcus Aurelius' great wars on the Danube, which in the event marked the beginning of the unrelenting barbarian pressure in the West, might, had not his death intervened, have led to his achieving his aim of conquering Central Europe north of the Danube. Instead, the year 180 saw the breakdown of the system of nominating successors to the imperial throne that had produced a century of moderate and extremely able emperors. The accession of Marcus' dreadful son, Commodus, coincided in Britain with the outbreak of the serious warfare in the north mentioned above. In Britain and elsewhere, attempts to tighten up discipline in the Roman army had ironic consequences. A short period that saw a return to a rapid succession of murdered emperors and fresh outbreaks of civil war ended not only with the army in a much stronger position in society but with other profound changes in the system. The final victor, after the defeat of Clodius Albinus in Gaul, was the immensely tough Septimius Severus. But, far from bringing the army back to the disciplined loyalty of the previous hundred years, Severus' strategy for the survival of his own dynasty was to subordinate everything to the interests of the troops.

The third-century emperors abandoned the pretence of rule by consent. The senatorial class, which the second-century emperors had, with varying degrees of sincerity, tried to keep involved in the responsibilities of government, both civil and military, lost ground to the career soldiers who were providing the professional officers whom the army increasingly required. The old distinction between Roman citizens and provincials without the citizenship, already fading as more and more of the latter won Roman status, was now swept away and replaced by a new class structure before the law—an upper division (*honestiores*) and a lower (*humiliores*). Significantly, soldiers fell into the former category. By the middle of the century, rampant inflation had severely damaged confidence in the currency; and the old economic pattern of major centres of production serving very large areas of the Roman world by means of long-distance trade based on a money economy was tending to be replaced by more localized industries.

For the first quarter of the third century, Septimius Severus and his dynasty seemed to offer a renewed stability, even if one based on military autocracy. But that in itself was an insecure foundation. In the middle of the century, one assassinated emperor followed another in rapid succession as army officers changed their allegiances. The old, fatal weaknesses of personal ambition and the readiness of the Roman soldier to follow his commander were unchecked. At this point almost total disaster struck as barbarians attacked in both East and West. In the East a newly-invigorated Persian Empire captured the Emperor Valerian, while successive Germanic invasions wrecked the unwalled cities of Gaul and prevented Rome from any more shielding her towns and territories across the Rhine with a permanent military presence. By 260 much of the empire was in a sorry state.

It was formerly believed that Britain had been similarly devastated when Clodius Albinus' unsuccessful campaign on the Continent against Severus was supposed to have stripped Britain of troops and opened the way for a major barbarian invasion. The archaeology will no longer support such a hypothesis. Problems with the tribes beyond the northern frontier towards the end of Severus' life did, however, give him a reason to choose Britain to launch a new war of conquest. There was no slackening of Roman ambition. Here the intention was the total subjugation of Scotland, to complete the conquest of the island. There is, indeed, cause to think that the interest of the Severan House in Britain revived a province that had become somewhat run down. Perhaps in connection with the imperial visit itself, London was tidied up, given new public buildings, provided with the longest circuit of walls in Britain and, at some time in the Severan period, its waterfront magnificently re-equipped with continuous quays running for more than half a mile. While the war was being planned, the imperial household itself probably settled at York. Much work had already been undertaken on the forts of the north behind the Wall, many of which seem to have been neglected, since the defeat of the barbarian intruders in the early 180s. There is some reason to think that York itself had assumed some of the governmental functions formerly located at London, perhaps when the Antonine reoccupation of Scotland extended the lines of communication. Sometime early in the third century the city that had grown up alongside the legionary fortress was dignified with the honorary rank of Roman colony. It is not, therefore, surprising to find London and York being chosen as twin capitals when, at some not entirely certain point in the Severan period, Britain was divided into two provinces. This was in line with a new policy to reduce the number of legions under the command of any one provincial governor and thus the temptation to revolt.

The planned conquest of Scotland was called off—but only after substantial successes—owing to the death of the emperor and the pressures on his successor. Security of the frontier was, however, accomplished. Britain as a whole shows every sign of having escaped the disasters of the age elsewhere. There was a slowing of new development, but the towns remained active and the villas were, if not expanded, kept up. Industry, if pottery is an indication, benefited from the problems of its

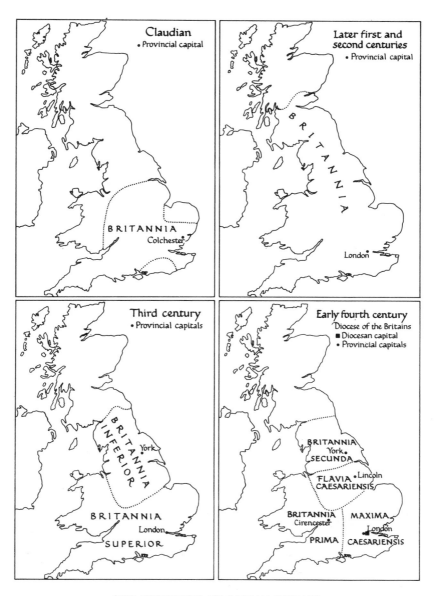

Claudian
• Provincial capital

BRITANNIA
Colchester

Later first and second centuries
• Provincial capital

BRITANNIA

London

Third century
• Provincial capitals

BRITANNIA INFERIOR
York

BRITANNIA
London
SUPERIOR

Early fourth century
Diocese of the Britains
■ Diocesan capital
• Provincial capitals

BRITANNIA
York
SECUNDA

FLAVIA
CAESARIENSIS
• Lincoln

BRITANNIA
Cirencester
MAXIMA

PRIMA
CAESARIENSIS
London

THE PROVINCES OF ROMAN BRITAIN

rivals on the Continent. Some public work that might have been expected was not undertaken: restoration in the Fenlands after severe flooding, for example. But the defences of Britain continued to be refurbished, and new forts built on the south and east coast, at Brancaster and Reculver, probably for purposes of political control of the routes to the Continent and not yet indicative of an acute threat from sea-borne barbarians. In Gaul, AD 260 saw yet more trouble from the Germans—not yet by any means the worst—and the central government in Rome lost control. Germany, Gaul, Spain, and Britain adhered to an independent emperor, comprising together the 'Empire of the Gallic Provinces' (*Imperium Galliarum*). This grouping had been foreshadowed under Clodius Albinus and re-emerged later as a structural part of the restored empire. For the time being, however, possession of peaceful, prosperous Britain with its powerful and undamaged forces and its almost legendary propaganda value must have been a considerable comfort to the Gallic emperors.

Britain under the Late Empire

In the 270s the imminent collapse of the empire—imminent, that is, with hindsight—was averted. Romans did not behave then or later as if Rome could ever fall. Emperors and would-be emperors or emperor-makers did not cease murdering one another, but a series of great soldier-emperors nevertheless restored the military balance against the barbarians, put down rival administrations, and began to repair the physical and institutional fabric of the State. This was done to such an effect that the imperial system was enabled to survive another two centuries in the West (and might have lasted much longer) and twelve in the East. In 274 Britain was brought back under the central government when the Emperor Aurelian eliminated the Gallic Empire. Britain's immediate fate, however, was very different from that of the Gallic part of the former independent north-western state. In 276 the towns of Gaul were still un-

walled when, as a literary source tells us, the worst of the barbarian invasions yet saw the capture of fifty or sixty towns and
their retaking by the Romans. In north-eastern France archaeology has revealed the abandonment in the late third century of
villa after villa in what had been a region outstanding for its
extraordinarily dense pattern of really large country houses and
their estates. These houses were not to be reoccupied.

In Britain the contrast is acute. In the period 250–70 there are
signs of a modest amount of building and none of universal
neglect, while archaeologists are tending to date an increasing
amount of new construction, particularly of villas or of enlargements and improvements to villas, to around 270–5—for example in the villas of Witcombe and Forcester Court, on the
western edge of the Cotswolds. An interesting hypothesis has
been advanced that there was a 'flight of capital' from Gaul to
Britain. There is no positive evidence for this theory yet, but if
modified a little it is attractive. It is certainly true that the great
age of the Romano-British villa, long recognized as being at its
peak in the fourth century, must have had its beginnings in the
270s. It seems unlikely, however, that landowners could have
'extracted their capital' from their ruined Gallic estates (in
other words, sold them at a good price). When these estates
were reoccupied at the end of the century it was as abandoned
land given over to settlers imported by government. Behind the
argument, however, lies too parochial a view of land own-
ership, an unspoken assumption that the typical provincial
landowner possessed a single estate and lived in its villa most of
the time. Possession of more than one estate was common
among the upper classes of the Roman world, where wealth
and status were quintessentially marked by landed property,
sometimes in many parts of the empire simultaneously. For the
pattern of Britain and Gaul at this period it is thus much more
likely that owners with land on both sides of the Channel
decided to transfer their personal residences from their Gallic
villas to their properties in what must have seemed an exceptionally secure haven in an age of extreme danger; and the

movement may already have started among the more cautious under the Gallic Empire. Perhaps a small piece of circumstantial evidence is that when the cities of Gaul finally were walled after 276, the circuits, though very strong, were in general short (quite unlike Britain), sometimes more like those of very powerful fortresses than walled towns. This is just what one would expect if there were no longer enough magnates with active local interests who could be tapped for the funds to defend the whole urban area.

Architecturally, the walls of these Gallic fortress cities do have close relations in Britain which are more or less contemporary, but they are not the towns. A number of new coastal fortresses were built in southern Britain—with the same pattern of very high stone walls and massive projecting towers—and older forts such as Brancaster and Reculver were modernized after the same fashion. At a much later date—in the fifth century—they are listed under a commander 'of the Saxon Shore', which has persistently suggested that they originated as a planned system of defence against Saxon sea-pirates. This is probably an anachronism. There is some reason to think that Aurelian's successor, Probus, created a tighter control of both sides of the Channel by establishing in Britain and Gaul similar strings of coastal forts; but the prime purpose has not been proven. The fact that Probus had more than once to quell serious moves against his authority in Britain may suggest that the 'Saxon Shore' had more at this stage to do with political security within the empire than frontier defence. Britain was an important asset—even more so in these straitened times—but control of the Channel was essential to its retention.

This fact was demonstrated in a remarkable fashion. In 287 a senior Roman officer named Carausius, who had been put in charge of a campaign to clear an infestation of pirates out of the Channel, came under strong suspicion of allowing the raids to happen and misappropriating the loot when it was subsequently seized by his fleet. Anticipating execution, Carausius rebelled and took control of Britain. Once again Britain was under the rule of a local emperor. This episode has attracted much romanticizing, but the fact is that neither Carausius nor other Romans before or after him who claimed the imperial title regarded Britain as something separate. Carausius is typical in blandly claiming on his coinage equality and fraternity with imperial colleagues, who, in fact, held the rest of the empire but with whom his fiction implied shared rule of the whole. The Carausian regime proved remarkably hard to dislodge, protected as it was by the sea. Carausius himself was unseated and murdered by Allectus, one of his own men, when he had lost a foothold on the Continent with the end of the siege of Boulogne in 293; but it was another three years before the central Roman government could launch a successful invasion. The Channel had proved formidable again.

Despite the fact that an element of inspired seamanship and a good deal of luck contributed greatly to the defeat of Allectus—not to mention what looks very much like lack of enthusiasm for his cause on the part of the regular garrison of Britain—in fact by 296 the rebel administration in Britain had faced a much more formidable central power. Major changes had taken place in the Roman State in those few years which move us into the period known as the 'Late Roman Empire'. The driving force was the Emperor Diocletian. Rooting himself in Roman precedent like Augustus, he initiated through his reforms a period of change that transformed the Roman State over half a century. He attempted to deal with the chronic political instability by creating a system of two senior emperors (*Augusti*) and two juniors as 'Caesars', with automatic succession. The individual provinces were once again reduced in size, and now grouped in 'dioceses', under a new tier of civilian officers known as *vicarii* to whom the governors (no longer commanding armies) were now made responsible. The frontiers were strengthened by approximately doubling the units of the army, under new commanders. Against domestic conspiracy or military revolt a deliberate attempt was made to create a greater aura around the persons of the emperors. The overall increases in the civil service were noted as phenomenal. The effects on art, fashion, and manners were hardly less pronounced.

The economic ravages of the century had been acute. Manpower shortages were now tackled by imposing rigid controls on the movement of labour, making many occupations hereditary. The problem was exceptionally severe on the land. There, the estate system which under the Late Republic had relied on a ready supply of cheap slaves from foreign wars had, in the course of the Early Empire, moved extensively to letting-out to large numbers of free tenant farmers on short leases. The disastrous economic conditions of the third century over large parts of the empire encouraged drift from the land. In reply, Diocletian virtually created a tied peasantry (the *coloni*) by law. Inflation was—ineffectually—tackled by detailed price legislation (on British duffel coats, rugs, and beer, for example). Persons in the public service were increasingly protected by being paid partially or wholly in kind. Troops, who had formerly had to buy their personal equipment out of their pay, were henceforth supplied from state factories, while officials' allowances came to be valued as much as their salaries. Taxation soared to meet the cost of reform; and the new rigidity of society had to be further tightened against attempted avoidance of the specific tax liabilities imposed on certain classes in the social hierarchy.

The new order must have arrived in full force in Britain soon after the reconquest in 296 by the Caesar in the West, Constantius I, the father of Constantine the Great. His timely rescue of London from a retreating force of Frankish mercenaries who had been in the pay of Allectus was a huge propaganda victory. It will be seen to be prophetic in more ways than one.

Most of the disorder seems to have been in the south, confined to the short campaign when Allectus was defeated. In the north, archaeological evidence for vigorous rebuilding of military installations initiated by Constantius seems more to indicate an intention for the future than repair of damage caused by enemies. The evidence suggests that a lengthy period of peace had allowed maintenance and manning to have low priority. Constantius had different ideas. Indeed, an unconvincing contemporary denial strengthens the impression that he had every intention, when opportunity offered, of launching another of those prestigious campaigns in Scotland that seem to have appealed so much to ambitious Roman emperors. Certainly, he lost no time after he became Augustus in preparing for such a war, and in 306 he was in the field. The sources claim a victory over the Picts (the first time the enemy in Scotland appears under this name); and pottery of the period found at Cramond at the eastern end of the Antonine Wall and from the old Severan fortress on the Tay suggests another sweep up the eastern side of the Highlands as his plan. Like Severus, Constantius returned to York and there died. Like Severus he had had his successor with him.

In the elevation of Constantine the Great by the army, York can fairly be said to have witnessed one of the turning-points in history. It was a curiously haphazard affair, strongly influenced by a German king called Crocus who had accompanied Constantius as one of his principal allies—and was completely contrary to the spirit of Diocletian's settlement. It set off a chain of events that ended with Constantine as sole emperor, putting into supreme power a man quite unlike Diocletian in having little adherence to the traditional past but like him capable of thinking and acting on the grandest scale. Constantine's innovations on the basis of Diocletian's conservative but immense reforms set patterns for centuries to come.

It has long been recognized that the first half of the fourth century was something of a 'golden age' for Roman Britain. We can now see that this was based on sound foundations from the previous century and continued trends already emerging in the 270s. This period of great prosperity certainly continued till the 340s, possibly till just after the middle of the century. It can legitimately be suspected that the most brilliant phase owed something to the favour of Constantine. There is some reason to suppose that, like his father, he too returned to Britain and celebrated military success here. We certainly know that for part of his reign he promoted to major status the mint at London that had been set up by Carausius. It is not impossible, too, that it was he who was responsible for changing London's name to 'Augusta'; and we may strongly suspect that the superb new river face of the walls of the fortress of York was a deliberate expression of the power of the man who had been proclaimed there, and who shared Hadrian's pleasure in vast architectural gestures.

The spirit of the age is typified by the great villas of fourth-century Britain. Socially and economically, the Late Empire in the West was marked by a polarization of wealth and to some extent power between the greater landed aristocracy on the one hand and emperor, court, and army on the other. These forces were often in conflict, but gradually tended to merge. Between them they left relatively little for the old urban middle class and the lesser gentry. Generally in the empire it was on the members of the local councils, the *curiales*, that the burden of paying for the new order fell most heavily. What had once been an honour now became a hereditary burden, and ways out were gradually sealed off by legislation.

Who, then, can have been the obviously wealthy inhabitants of the larger Romano-British villas? Some may have been rich citizens who had transferred themselves from elsewhere. If senators, or imperial officials of appropriate standing, they will have been exempt from the duties of *curiales*. Yet the curious persistence in Britain of forms of Latin indicative of educated speech but tending to be peculiar to the island does suggest that the native aristocracy remained a significant element in society. It is highly probable that they had, exceptionally, not been too badly hit in the previous century. It is tempting to wonder too, whether Constantine may not have shown them special favour.

Like the eighteenth-century English country house, to which they may in many respects reasonably be compared, these villas vary in plan, complexity, and size. Certain features are generally present—notably, construction in permanent materials, central heating (in the form of wood-, sometimes coal-fired hot-air systems), glazing, tessellated floors, and very often one or more complete bath suites. Agricultural buildings normally adjoin, and like their Georgian counterparts it is probable that most had land attached. It is clear from Roman literature that the degree and importance to the individual occupier of any particular villa of its 'economic' activity could vary enormously, from being a major source of income to little more than an amusement. Significantly, the great houses such as Woodchester, Chedworth, or North Leigh did not stand alone, but formed the top of a very broad pyramid of villas. The modest villas that had developed in earlier times out of Iron Age farms survived, improved, or were replaced by new middle-range and small villas. This is the best evidence for the survival of a solid gentry in Britain. Some villas, it is true, disappear; but this is in the natural order of things even in a completely settled age. It is more important that in this age the villa is becoming a more prominent feature of the landscape, not less.

It has been observed that villas often display duplication in their main facilities. This has led to a somewhat complicated hypothesis to suggest that surviving Celtic custom caused a widespread shared (or divided) use of one complex by two families or two owners. An infinitely simpler explanation is that in the Roman world a gentleman of any consequence travelled with a considerable retinue of servants and friends, and that visiting one another's country houses was part of the regular social round. For journeys, the reputation of inns was so evil that anyone with the right connections preferred to travel by moving from one acquaintance's villa to another. Most Romano-British villas seem to have been connected by a drive or lane to a public road and the majority were within ten miles or so of a town. Their social relationships to the towns, and perhaps even more to one another, are therefore likely to have been as important as their economic effects.

How much the development of the large villas changed the agricultural scene we do not know. As early as the second century an occasional pattern of villa and village has been observed which seems not unlike that of manor house and village in later ages. It may be that in fourth-century Britain there were comparatively few Diocletianic *coloni*—or that changes in the law made little difference to a situation that had long existed in this relatively undisturbed region of the empire. Small, native-style farms are still much in the majority, though there are some signs of consolidation into larger units. A greater change was the encouragement given to the various trades that served the decoration of the great houses. The best known of these are the regional 'schools' of mosaicists—firms or groups of firms with workshops centred respectively on Cirencester, Chesterton (Water Newton), Dorchester (Dorset), Brough-on-Humber, and somewhere centrally in the south. Other trades, working in more perishable materials, perhaps operated in similar fashion—for example fresco-painters (of whose work just enough survives to demonstrate its importance and the quality it could reach); furniture-makers; and other suppliers of major items for the well-to-do household.

The ancient countryside was not exclusively agricultural—nor only for the pleasure of the rich. The falling-off of long-distance trade in the third century had given encouragement to more than one British industry, for example the vast potteries of the Nene Valley. In the fourth century we can observe how a similarly huge ceramic industry in Hampshire which had also expanded in the third century—mostly within the area of the later royal forest of Alice Holt—now captured the London market and flourished greatly.

In these early years of the Late Roman period the principal features of the administrative system had emerged into which the new-style provincial governors fitted. Ultimate decisions might emanate from Milan (which emperors had for some time found more convenient than Rome) or, after 324, Constantinople. But from the time of Constantius I, the central government was for routine purposes situated at Trier, on the Moselle. The head of the civil administration as far as Britain was concerned

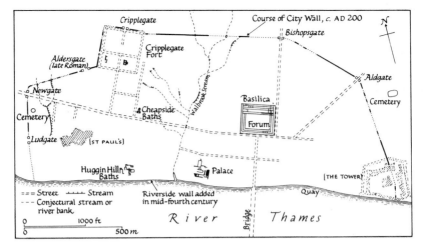

ROMAN LONDON

was the praetorian prefect of the Gauls, based in Trier, to whom the *vicarius* of the British diocese was responsible. The prefecture grouped together Britain, Spain, and northern and southern Gaul. The headquarters of the British *vicarius* was almost certainly in London. Under him were four provincial governors—of Maxima Caesariensis (also probably based in London), Britannia Prima (Cirencester), Flavia Caesariensis (Lincoln?), and Britannia Secunda (York?), each with his own staff. As well as normal civil duties, this structure had a vital military role in being in charge of supply, including the new state factories (a weaving-mill of the sort that supplied the Late Roman army with material for uniforms is, for example, recorded in Britain). A fifth-century document, showing unusual insignia for the *vicarius* of the Britons, may denote that by that time at least he had, exceptionally, some troops under his command. More important is the fact that with supply in civilian hands there was some potential check on the army. Socially the senior members of this new administration were drawn from the educated middle and upper part of Roman society. The British vicariate could be an important stage in a fully professional career, and the men in the post of whom we know were not mediocrities. Into the beginning of the fifth century it remained policy not to employ men in their own provinces in senior posts, and most would expect to serve at some stage at the imperial court.

The financial administration of the provinces was very different from that in the Early Empire. Though the financial headquarters was again in London, the old provincial procurators had disappeared. The governors of the individual British provinces were responsible to the *vicarius* for the taxation in kind which the municipal councils were expected to raise from the individual taxpayer. Independent of the *vicarius*, however, were two other separate financial departments each with a diocesan chief officer, eventually responsible directly to the imperial secretariat. One handled taxation in cash, controlled the issue of coinage, and administered mines and certain other operations. The other was responsible for crown property throughout Britain, and to it reported the local procurators who acted as agents in charge. These two branches, however, often worked closely together and could call on the assistance of provincial governors to carry out their functions in the field.

The command structure for the army no longer had to correspond with provinces. At the same time the old distinction between legions and auxiliaries was replaced by a new one categorizing units into garrison, or frontier, troops (*limitanei*) and new, mobile field forces (*comitatenses*), the latter having higher status and remuneration. Many of the old units retained their identity, especially in Britain, where much of the old frontier remained substantially unchanged even if the internal character of units altered. At this time, the units stationed in Britain were classified as *limitanei*, emphasizing its character as a region to be defended rather than a place from which a field army might rapidly be deployed. The commander of a garrison army was entitled *dux*—the *dux Britanniarum* being one such. Mobile forces, on the other hand, tended to be led by a *comes rei militaris*, of superior rank. Under Constantine himself there was only one central field army. But under his warring sons several major field armies emerged, under generals of even higher rank. Certain of these army groups achieved permanence; and smaller task forces drawn from them became operative under such *comites rei militaris.*

The field armies contained both old units that had been retained or reformed and many new ones. Among the latter, an important proportion was raised from peoples of Germanic origin; and in the fourth century there were also many individual German recruits. Something like half the regular army in the West was German, and half Roman, including the officer corps. In 367 the *dux Britanniarum* defeated by barbarians, for example, was named Fullofaudes. By the end of the century, German generals were occupying the very highest commands. Though it was no longer fashionable for such men to adopt Roman names, they fully absorbed the attitudes and ambitions of their native-born Roman equals. However, as a group the fourth-century army officers tended to be noticeably different, culturally, from their counterparts of equivalent rank in the civil service. Important cultural prejudices, not to say dislike and contempt, appeared between certain emperors and their officers on the one hand and leading civilians on the other; and stresses between emperors, their courts, and their new capitals, and the old aristocracy that still looked towards Rome, became socially and politically important.

The final element in the Constantinian equation was the Church. The traditional public religion of the Roman State had sufficed for public purposes, but offered little to the individual. The breakdown of the Antonine peace and the crises of the third century coincided with a widespread desire for a more personal religion that offered consolation and meaning in this world and a better life in the next. Concomitantly, close contact with the East brought about the spread of various Eastern 'mystery religions', religions offering mystic revelation and personal contact with a deity. Hadrian himself had worshipped at the ancient shrine of the Eleusinian mysteries in Greece and a variety of mystery religions became respectable and accepted. The Persian cult of Mithras gained a powerful hold in military and commercial circles, where its insistence on high standards of probity and discipline and its tightly-bound brotherhood matched the ideals and interests of businessmen and officers. Unlike Christianity it was not politically suspect, and therefore not persecuted. In Britain, its chapels appear exclusively where the army or trading community were strong—at Rudchester, Carrawburgh, or Housesteads on Hadrian's Wall, and in London. Its weakness was its very exclusivity, closed to women and largely restricted to one social class. Its rites were sufficiently close to those of Christianity to make them appear blasphemous, and there are possible signs in London and at Carrawburgh, for example, of Christian attack during the Christian ascendancy, and it largely faded away during the fourth century.

Recent work on the survival of Roman Christianity in Britain after the end of Roman rule has suggested that it was more widespread and deeply-rooted than was formerly thought. It is important, however, not to read too much back from the fifth and sixth centuries into the third and fourth. It is generally agreed that Christianity had little hold in Britain before the fourth century. Third-century Britain had, indeed, its martyrs—St. Alban at Verulamium, SS Julius and Aaron probably at Caerleon. The fact that Britain fell in the part of the empire ruled by Constantius I, whose former wife was St. Helena, mother of Constantine, and who permitted the last great persecution to go no further in his area than the demolition of churches, may have had the negative effect of preventing a substantial early martyr cult in Britain. On the other hand, it may also have attracted well-to-do Christians to transfer their residences from more dangerous parts of the empire, unobtrusively increasing the villa-dwelling population.

Britain has produced the earliest set of church plate yet known from the Roman Empire (from Water Newton), almost certainly very early fourth century in date, while British bishops appear only a year after the 'Edict of Milan' legalized the Church, bearing titles indicating as their sees the capitals of the four British provinces. These facts draw our attention to the fundamental change that came with Constantine the Great. The growth of absolutism in the third century had been accompanied by sporadic imperial attempts to introduce a monotheistic state religion. From the time of Constantine the central new factor in Roman politics (and increasingly in the private sphere as well) was ideology. It was no longer sufficient to observe the customary formalities of the state religion to demonstrate loyalty: Christianity, as the new state religion, required belief. Toleration of pagan practices lasted for long. But it was gradually withdrawn, despite intense opposition during the whole of the fourth century from a powerful section of the Roman aristocracy, who both saw the old religion as central to Rome herself, and identified with it in opposition to the court. There were even to be short periods when there were pagan emperors again, sympathetic to them. Within the Church itself, however, there was a further development of immense significance for its future when the Emperor Constantius II decided that it was an imperial duty to ensure unity on doctrine. From the middle of the fourth century the hunting of heresy by the State added a new dimension to the politics of loyalty.

What must, therefore, surprise us in Britain is not that recent research has indicated a considerable amount of Christianization in the fourth century, but that there is not more. This will lead us to examine the apparent nature of the British church. The old notion of urban Christianity and rural paganism certainly cannot be sustained. Urban communities under Constantine are suggested by the bishops mentioned. A very small and unusual church excavated inside the walls at Silchester, and probable examples of the much more common cemetery churches over the graves of martyrs and other prominent Christians at Verulamium, Canterbury, and elsewhere, all point in the same direction. But the grand monuments of fourth-century Romano-British Christianity are associated with the villas:

mosaics at Frampton and Hinton St. Mary, for example, or the wall-paintings of Lullingstone. The distribution of archaeological evidence suggests that the incidence of Christianity was very patchy. A cemetery at Dorchester in Dorset indicates a large and wealthy Christian community, supported by the surrounding villas; elsewhere similar cemeteries have nothing. A remarkable series of lead baptismal fonts has not come from cities but rural locations or small settlements, likely to have been under the eye of the landowning gentry, and a very substantial proportion of them has been found in East Anglia, where there is evidence of real personal wealth in the Late Roman period.

Constantine had dealt a massive blow both to the pagan cults and to the municipalities by distributing the endowments and treasures of the temples to the Church and by diverting funds from the civic treasuries. Wealth in the fourth century increasingly fell into the hands of the greater landowners, on the one hand, and of the State and its institutions, on the other. In Britain, where the villas are such an outstanding feature of the period, it is not surprising to find them in the forefront of the development of Christianity. Nor, under these circumstances, is it surprising to find the evidence so patchy. If the strength of Christianity in a district depended on whether the local landowner was an enthusiastic Christian (or politically ambitious) or not, then this is exactly what we might predict. If the erection of churches and other Christian monuments had depended on an energetic town council, as had the provision of public temples and other civic amenities in earlier periods, then the provision might have been relatively more even. It is clear that substantially more bishops from Britain were present at the Council of Rimini in 359, but no titles survive and it is therefore not known whether they were city-based. It is perhaps significant that some, at least, were known to have had difficulty in raising the money to pay their travelling expenses. If, then, the urban Christian communities were weak—or declined over the century after an initial Constantinian boost—what does this imply for the survival of Christianity after the end of Roman rule? The clue is perhaps the eventual reconciliation to Christianity of the landowning class as a whole elsewhere in the West, if it was paralleled in fifth-century Britain. In that period, quite unlike the fourth century, we ought to see a fairly uniform spread of Christianity among the rural population. Since most of the population had, anyhow, always lived on the land, that ought to lead us to expect the general persistence of Christianity, at least as a subculture. Indeed, the fact that in Late Roman times the rural clergy, unlike their urban counterparts, were relatively poorly educated and socially obscure (in the country, even bishops could be little more than dependants of landowners), may have assisted their identification with the agricultural multitude and ensured the survival of a Church as well as a faith, whatever eventually happened to the landed proprietors themselves.

How long did the villa-based society of the fourth century retain its brilliant early prosperity, so different from so many other parts of the empire? Describing a series of raids by barbarians on places near the frontiers of Britain in AD 360, the well-informed contemporary historian, Ammianus, tells us that at that time 'a pall of fear lay over the provinces' and adds, significantly, that they 'were already exhausted by the accumulation of disaster over the years'. The opinion, moreover, has been advanced, based on the archaeology of the towns, that the latter were 'finished' by about 350 (an opinion which we shall have to interpret later). Details apart, however, the picture is startlingly different from the earlier years of the century.

There is good reason to think that the 'golden age' did not long outlive Constantine himself. His death in 337 left the empire uneasily divided between three sons, Constantius II, Constans, and Constantine II. Britain came within the dominions of the younger Constantine. Dissatisfied with his share, he attacked Constans in 340 and suffered total defeat. It was a long time since the army of Britain had been involved in a military disaster. Subsequent weakness—and possibly disaffection—are probably reflected in a most unusual and un-expected journey across the winter Channel by Constans in person in 343, the brief surviving references to which hint at pressures on the northern frontier. Border problems were certainly acute by 360, the moment to which our quotation from Ammianus refers, when Scots from Ireland and Picts from Scotland had broken an agreement with Rome, implying that there had been earlier threats settled by diplomacy (and probably, in the usual style, with gold). In 364 they were back time and time again, now accompanied by 'Attacotti', probably also from Ireland, and by Saxons. The great barbarian invasion of 367, to which we shall come, was therefore the culmination of a long period of trouble from outside. But events at least as bad had occurred inside the territory under Roman rule.

In 350 a palace conspiracy ended in the murder of Constans and the elevation of an officer of Germanic descent named Magnentius. The Western part of the empire was now at war with the East, under the surviving son Constantius II. The three-and-a-half-year rule of Magnentius, Christian but tolerant of pagans, proved disastrous in its consequences. Constantius II, whom we have already seen assuming the duty of suppressing Christian heresies, also hated paganism—indeed he reintroduced the death penalty for its observance and scandalized the senate by removing the ancient Altar of Victory from the Senate House in Rome. With his final victory, Britain came under special scrutiny. The appointment of the head of the imperial establishment records office, one Paulus, was made with the aim of hunting down dissidents in the island. Black humour aptly nicknamed him 'The Chain'. His brief was to arrest certain military men who had supported Magnentius, but he soon extended this, unchecked, into a reign of terror in which false evidence played a dominant part, horrifying even the most loyal officers. Constantius' own *vicarius* of Britain, Martinus, sacrificed himself in a brave but unsuccessful attempt to put an end to Paulus. One cannot but suspect that many leading families which had been implicated in incidents in the past half-century were drawn into this whirlpool, in addition to those involved in current politics. Confiscations, exile, imprisonment, torture, and executions were approved by the emperor without any questioning of the evidence. The confiscations of property alone must have had a profound effect on the landed prosperity of Britain, while the devastation of morale among both civilians and army can only have left them in a weaker state to resist the barbarian troubles now pressing in on them.

The nadir came in 367. Picts, Scots, and Attacotti invaded Britain; Franks and Saxons attacked the coast of Gaul. Both the central imperial command—the Emperor Valentinian himself was in northern Gaul—and the senior officers responsible for Britain were taken by surprise. The *dux* in command of the static garrison of Britain was put out of action and the *comes* in charge of coastal defence killed. The most remarkable feature was the concerted action of such disparate barbarians. Treachery by native frontier scouts in the north is one attested part of the situation, but to account for the total operation we have to suppose an unknown barbarian with extraordinary military and diplomatic ability. Detailed knowledge of Roman dispositions and understanding of Roman military methods were not hard to come by, with so many Germans in the Roman army (though conscious disloyalty to Rome is very rarely indeed to be suspected). What convinces one of inspired barbarian leadership is the fact of simultaneous attacks by peoples with very different cultures, from homelands relatively distant from one another, with a very clever division of targets—and, perhaps most of all, with the maintenance of complete secrecy. The Romans certainly called it a conspiracy, and it is difficult not to agree with them.

Once in Britain, the barbarians ranged unchecked in small bands, looting, destroying, taking prisoners, or killing at will. The countryside near to roads must have been particularly vulnerable and not all walled towns seem to have resisted. Both civil authority and military discipline broke down. Troops deserted, some claiming—unconvincingly—to be on leave.

Political opportunists seized their chances. Britain was being used as a place of dignified exile for high-ranking offenders, and one well-documented conspiracy among them was nipped in the bud just after the Roman recovery of Britain. But there is also some evidence that one of the provinces of the British diocese (which had now been divided into five, rather than four) fell temporarily into the hands of rebels.

The response of Valentinian to the calamity was the dispatch of a small but powerful task force of élite troops under a *comes rei militaris*, Theodosius, who was the father of the later Emperor Gratian and grandfather of Theodosius the Great, and whose own father had himself served as a *comes* in Britain, under Constans. Such task forces became a frequent method of dealing with emergencies under the Late Empire: Britain had at least once already been the scene of such an expedition (in 360), possibly more than once. At this time these forces were usually made up of *comitatenses*. From the end of the fourth century, barbarian war bands under their own kings, even whole tribes, became more and more often accepted into Roman armies. Task forces thereafter tended to be made up of a mixture of whatever regular troops could be found and barbarian allies, or sometimes barbarians alone on contract for a specific campaign or operation. Looking forward, it is important to realize that in the fifth century, as military practice evolved out of that of the fourth century, 'the barbarians' were not like some hostile aliens from outer space but were a familiar fact of life. Barbarian warriors were frequently employed against other barbarians in the suppression of internal disorder, and for the prosecution of Roman civil wars.

Theodosius' conduct of the campaign and subsequent reconstruction of Britain seems to have been both brilliant and thorough. London was spectacularly relieved. Garrison troops were reassembled, deserters pardoned, and an effective army recreated. The barbarian war parties on land were picked off one by one and the Saxons defeated at sea. Goods stolen from the provincials were recovered and returned. Civil authority was restored under a new *vicarius*; the province that had been lost to rebels was regained and named Valentia in honour of Valentinian, and his eastern colleague and brother, Valens. Forts were rebuilt and damaged cities restored.

The extensive remodelling of town defences in Britain by the addition of prominent external towers, dated archaeologically to somewhere in the middle of the fourth century, is more convincingly to be attributed to Theodosius' initiative than to any other, although the variety in design and arrangement does suggest that, once again, the cost and responsibility fell on the local councillors. However, the fact that it is always the full circuit that was retained in use has very important implications for the state of the towns in the middle and late fourth century. Such wide circuits cannot have been kept solely to provide military strong points or even as refuges in time of danger for a dispersed rural population. There was something worthwhile defending with permanent works. What, then, are we to make of the notion that the towns of Britain were 'finished' by about 350? The unspoken assumption that fourth-century towns were of the same sort as those of the second is clearly mistaken. We have, of course, to be careful not to assume that all towns changed in the same ways. Yet the decay or disuse of civic public buildings is hardly surprising in the context of municipal treasuries raided by central government and councils made up of now unwilling members. Fourth-century legislation repeatedly tried to prevent members of the class that now had the hereditary obligation to serve from moving their main residences away from the towns, while those in higher social classes were exempt from municipal obligations. The new element in society was the vastly-expanded bureaucracy, and it is in their direction that we should probably be looking. Five governors, their staffs, households, companies of guards, and the many others connected with them needed housing; and there were numerous other officials with inflated establishments and life-styles supported by substantial allowances. At each level in the hierarchies, expectations existed which in the end filtered down from the lavish grandeur of the Late Roman court. Large areas of fourth-century capitals such as Trier or Arles, once normal municipalities, were given over to palaces and other associated official buildings. On a smaller scale, we ought to expect such a pattern in many towns in Britain. In fact, archaeology has demonstrated the building of large town houses in places as different as London and Carmarthen, and urban development into the middle of the fifth century at Verulamium and, of a distinctive sort, at Wroxeter. In the cultivated open spaces of this period observed within the city walls in excavations we should perhaps see the gardens and grounds of the new-style establishment rather than a decay represented by abandoned building sites. Indeed, in London and York at least we may reasonably expect the presence of emperors themselves from time to time to have made a mark on the archaeological record.

There is no reason to think that the Theodosian restoration was other than outstandingly successful. Archaeologically, it is clear that many villas continued in occupation; some were enlarged and others built from scratch. Hadrian's Wall was occupied to the end of Roman rule, even if individual garrisons were smaller than before. A new system of signal stations was established on the north-east coast. Much industry had been interrupted by the war of 367, but the many changes in pattern after it indicate vigour and new initiatives. Not surprisingly, some pagan religious sites disappear, but others continue in cult use, while still others show signs of conversion to new uses, some perhaps Christian, towards the end of the century. The forty years from 369 do not have the brilliance of the early fourth century, but the island does not provide any evidence for the sort of despair that the historians report for the 50s and 60s. In order to understand what happened in 409 it is important to realize that in the last part of the fourth century Roman Britain had not been running rapidly downhill.

This period is, in fact, marked by two more occasions on which major attempts on the imperial throne were launched from a base in Britain. In 382 a victory over the Picts by a general named Magnus Maximus (Macsen Wledig in Welsh legend) created for him a reputation that led to proclamation as emperor and the rule, for five years, of the part of the empire represented by the Gallic prefecture—Britain, Gaul, and Spain. In Britain, some forts, notably in the Pennines and Wales, were abandoned at this time and the Twentieth legion was withdrawn from Chester, but it remains still entirely uncertain whether Maximus' campaigns and eventual defeat at the hands of the Emperor Theodosius the Great had any significant overall effect on the defensive capability of the army in Britain. Between 392 and 394 Britain was peripherally involved in another palace revolt for the duration of which Theodosius lost control of the Western empire, but the significance of this incident lies more in the appearance of a general, a Frank in this case, overshadowing a compliant emperor in the West. The death of Theodosius in 395 made this new balance of power in the Western imperial government the rule, rather than the exception, for the rest of its history. The joint accession of Theodosius' sons, Honorius in the West, and Arcadius in the East, inaugurated a period in which the pattern of government in the two halves of the empire diverged fundamentally. In the East, it remained firmly in the hands of the emperor, or his chief civilian minister. In the West a powerful landed aristocracy, rooted in its estates, vied for influence with the professional soldiers who commanded the armies. After three-quarters of a century, both these parties were to come to the conclusion that they could manage without an emperor in the West.

The End of Roman Rule

The effective control of the West by the late Emperor Theodosius' chief lieutenant, Flavius Stilicho, Vandal by birth, was accompanied by a claim to the East as well. Plot, counterplot, and civil war between Stilicho, Honorius, the Western senate, and the Goths under Alaric did much to ensure in the long term the collapse of Roman rule throughout the West. In Britain, initial successes against Picts, Scots, and Saxons, and restoration of defences under Stilicho's direction were probably followed at the very beginning of the fifth century by some posting elsewhere of troops. We do not know the extent of the postings, but the cessation of bulk import of new coinage in 402 must mean that neither remaining regular troops nor civil officials were henceforth paid from central sources. It is not surprising that we find a mood of extreme discontent. In 406 the army in Britain elevated the first in a rapid succession of three emperors. On the last day of that year, large numbers of barbarians crossed the Rhine. The central government withdrew the administration of the prefecture of the Gauls to Arles, and had no time to deal with usurpers in Britain.

The third usurper ran true to form, seizing Gaul and Spain, and for some while was recognized as a legitimate colleague by the unwilling Honorius. Once again, we do not know if there was an overall reduction in the garrison of Britain, but some further withdrawal of regular units seems likely. The northwestern empire of Constantine III, however, was to be the last of its kind, and before it was finally extinguished Britain had ceased for ever to be under any sort of imperial rule.

We know tantalizingly little about the process by which this happened, but something can be pieced together. In 408 the absence of the bulk of Constantine's army in Spain left him unable to deal with heavy barbarian attacks on Britain. In 409 the mutiny of that army under its British-born commander (and his deliberate incitement of the barbarians in Gaul) coincided with renewed assaults on Britain by enemies who included Saxons. At this point, Britain, too—along with parts of Gaul—rebelled, expelling Constantine's administration. Britain successfully took on the barbarian invaders, and henceforth broke decisively with Roman rule.

How Britain expelled the invaders and what was then the state of the country can only be the subject of informed speculation. There are slight hints that Stilicho and Honorius had taken some steps to encourage local organization of, or payment for, defence. It is most unlikely that the regular army was retained when Constantine's officers were deposed, or that the elaborate administrative structure which supported it was manned and paid. Under the Late Empire, the landed class strongly resisted both the conscription of the agricultural labour force into the regular army and the payment of taxes. Elsewhere in the fifth century units whose pay stopped disbanded and dispersed or settled on the land. Indeed, from AD 455 the final running-down of the Western regular army seems to have been in progress. In Britain, with no central government, it is all the more likely that in the years from 409 groups of barbarians were paid to undertake the fighting, and some of these may already have been brought in under Constantine III or even Stilicho.

There is no sound reason for thinking that the Britons elevated any more emperors, or re-created any of the mechanisms of central government. Not only had very few of them had experience of senior office (unlike recent Gallo-Romans), but if they shared the sentiments of the landed class elsewhere in the fifth-century West, they are most unlikely to have wanted to reassume the burdens of supporting the system of imperial administration once they had been rid of it. The critical success of the Flavian governors of Britain in the first century had been to convince the native aristocracy that its advantage lay with Rome. There is no good reason to think that the events of 409 had destroyed the position of the landowning class. They are, however, very likely indeed by now to have lost confidence in the system of emperor, bureaucracy, and army as the best way of securing their still prosperous way of life. They will not have been encouraged by the ruthless political persecution in Gaul by Honorius' officers after the fall of Constantine III.

The presence of a full paper establishment of military and civil posts for Britain in the *Notitia Dignitatum* suggests that into the fifth century it was assumed centrally in the imperial ministries that Britain would be recovered—as it had so often

been in the past. There was, in fact, only one short period, from
425 to 429, when a Roman military intervention in Britain was
again a serious possibility. But by that time other groups of
well-to-do Roman provincials, particularly in a large area of
Gaul, were starting to settle down tolerably comfortably, em-
ploying, in alliance with, or under the rule of, barbarians.

Provided that the barbarians remained amenable, any of
these arrangements might suit the gentry better than direct
imperial rule. But for the weakened middle and artisan classes,
who in the fourth century had depended more and more on the
army, civil service, and urban church for jobs, patronage, or
markets, the change must have been disastrous. In Britain, the
Roman archaeology supports such a picture. Early in the fifth
century, the massive pottery industry comes to an apparently
abrupt end; by 420–30 coinage ceases to be in regular use.
These facts, incidentally, make the dating of the end of the
occupation of Roman sites in the fifth century much more
difficult than in earlier periods. There is, however, certainly no
evidence for villas having come generally to a violent end. Signs
of how late towns might be active vary a good deal. At Lincoln
we find a main street being resurfaced well into the fifth century; in London imported Mediterranean pottery in the ash of
the heating system of one house combines with other evidence
to suggest normal occupation in the early fifth century; the
forum at Cirencester was being kept up after the cessation of
general circulation of coins; and at Verulamium a sequence of
important buildings succeeding one another on the same site is
closed, strikingly, by the laying of a new water-main at a time
that cannot be far short of the middle of the century.

After the break with Rome the Britons, we are told, lived
under *tyranni*, or 'usurpers', best interpreted as local potentates
who had filled the vacuum left by the removal of legitimate
authority. Their background was probably very varied, some
perhaps landowners, others military men, Roman or barbarian,
who had been invited to take control or seized power. At
Gloucester, a rich warrior burial is British in character rather

than Saxon, and may represent a *tyrannus*, or a *condottiere* in local pay. At Wroxeter, ambitious fifth-century timber buildings may well represent the headquarters of such a leader.

In 429 St. Germanus, a prominent Gallo-Roman bishop who moved in high Roman circles, visited Britain to combat heresy, debating publicly with British magnates at Verulamium 'conspicuous for their riches, brilliant in dress, and surrounded by a fawning multitude'. The visit to Britain he repeated around 446/7, though apparently in deteriorating circumstances. At least until the 440s, therefore, something survived in Britain that was very like 'post-Roman' or 'post-imperial' life elsewhere in the West.

2. The Anglo-Saxon Period

(c.440–1066)

JOHN BLAIR

The Age of the Settlements

THE sources for the fifth and sixth centuries are so few that they can all be listed here, and so unsatisfactory that their faults must be clearly stated. On the one hand is the archaeological evidence, mainly objects from graves in pagan cemeteries. This evidence cannot lie, but the questions which it answers are strictly limited. On the other hand is a small group of texts, annals, and fragments. Of these the only substantial contemporary work is *The Ruin of Britain*, a tract written in the 540s by a British monk named Gildas whose purpose was to denounce the evils of his day in the most violent possible language. The Venerable Bede, a monk in the Northumbrian monastery of Jarrow, completed his great *Ecclesiastical History of the English People* in 731. This overshadows all other sources for the seventh and early eighth centuries, and although the invasion period was remote from Bede's own day he provides some surprisingly well-founded scraps of tradition. The only other narrative sources are fragments of chronicles preserved in later compilations, a few poems, and passing references by Continental writers. Of a very different kind are the late Saxon annals known collectively as *The Anglo-Saxon Chronicle*, which give a year-by-year summary of events in the southern English kingdoms. The early annals are much less reliable than those for later centuries, and their chronological framework is suspect before the late sixth century.

Thus there is no near-contemporary source of Anglo-Saxon origin. The reason is obvious enough: the Germanic peoples were illiterate during their first two centuries in Britain. So their early fortunes can only be glimpsed through the hostile eyes of Britons, through the ill-informed eyes of foreigners, and by means of their own half-remembered traditions. Until the late sixth century, informed guesswork must make do for history.

Archaeology provides the first clue, for it shows that there were Germanic warriors in Britain some years before 410. Late Roman cemeteries, especially along the Lower Thames Valley from Oxfordshire to the Essex coast, have produced burials with belt-fittings of a type worn by Frankish and Saxon mercenaries in the Roman army. If such troops were settled in Britain, as they certainly were in Gaul, the mid-fifth-century invaders may have joined relatives who had come two or three generations back. Sunken huts with gable-posts are characteristic of English settlement in the fifth and sixth centuries, and over two hundred of these have been found at a huge site near Mucking on the Thames estuary. It has been suggested that this complex housed mercenaries who were settled in *c*.400 to guard the approach to London. If so, the continuous history of Anglo-Saxon settlement begins under Roman rule.

The English of later centuries dated their ancestors' arrival some decades after this, and it does seem to have been from the 430s onwards that Germanic settlers arrived in large numbers. Before considering this remarkable process, it must be asked who the invaders were and what they were like. The first question is answered, almost as well as any modern scholar can answer it, in a startlingly well-informed passage quoted by Bede from an unknown source:

They came from three very powerful Germanic tribes, the Saxons, Angles and Jutes. The people of Kent and the inhabitants of the Isle of Wight are of Jutish origin, and also those opposite the Isle of Wight, that part of the kingdom of Wessex which is still today called the

nation of the Jutes. From the Saxon country, that is, the district now
known as Old Saxony, came the East Saxons, the South Saxons and
the West Saxons. Besides this, from the country of the Angles, that is,
the land between the kingdoms of the Jutes and the Saxons, which is
called *Angulus*, came the East Angles, the Middle Angles, the Mercians, and all the Northumbrian race (that is those people who dwell
north of the River Humber) as well as the other Anglian tribes.
Angulus is said to have remained deserted from that day to this.

Archaeology confirms Bede's analysis: objects found in English graves are comparable to those from North Germany and
the southern half of the Danish peninsula. Some urns from the
fifth-century cremation cemeteries in East Anglia may even be
work of the same potters as urns found in Saxony, and Kentish
pottery and jewellery resembles material from Jutland. A district north-east of Schleswig is called to this day Angeln. To
Bede's list we can probably add Frisians, mixed with Saxons
who seem to have been infiltrating the coastal settlements of
Frisia in the early fifth century. Even Bede's statement that
some of the homeland settlements were deserted is confirmed
by excavations at Feddersen Wierde, near the mouth of the
Weser. Here a village of large timber buildings was abandoned
in *c*.450, apparently in consequence of rising sea-levels. With
the natural fertility of lowland Britain, and the evidence that its
inhabitants deliberately imported mercenaries, this flooding of
coastal settlements helps to provide an explanation for the
Migrations.

Bede's racial division of the kingdoms of his own day is
probably over-neat. The men of Kent may well have been
mainly Jutish, and the other major peoples certainly thought
themselves either 'Angles' or 'Saxons'. But archaeology does
not suggest a very firm distinction, and by the late sixth century, when the kingdoms emerge into the light of day, there is
much blurring at the edges. Thus, the finest metalwork of the
East Angles resembles that of Kent, and their royal dynasty
seems to have been Swedish. Sea-passage must have weakened
ethnic ties, and new types of settlement and social organization

apparently developed to suit the needs of pioneer colonists. It is worth noting, for instance, the contrast between the large rectangular halls at Feddersen Wierde and the formless clusters of little sunken huts which are found on English sites. What mattered was not so much that the settlers were Angles, Saxons, or Jutes, as that they belonged to the same broad culture as southern Scandinavia, Germany, and northern France. Their earliest known poems include hero-legends set in Denmark and Frisia; an early seventh-century East Anglian king possessed Swedish and Gaulish treasures; and Christianity reached England through a Kentish king's marriage with a Frankish princess. Britain exchanged the Roman Empire for another, if very different, international community.

What were these people like? Obviously they were far less civilized than the Romans, yet they had their own institutions which proved astonishingly tough. Much that the first-century historian Tacitus wrote of the *Germani* applies to their distant descendants in England. As with the *Germani*, so throughout Anglo-Saxon history, the strongest social bonds were the claims of kinship and the claims of lordship.

Kin-groups were close-knit in the homeland, and they remained so in England. The families and dependants of one man may sometimes have formed their own settlement units, with shared resources and systems of land-allotment. The influence of such extended 'affinities' on the character of the settlements is shown by the numerous place-names ending -*ing*, -*ingham*, and -*ington*. Hastings means 'the people of Haesta', Reading 'the people of Reada', Wokingham 'the farm of Wocca's people', and so on. Although it is now thought that not all of these names belong to the first settlement phase, many are early and important and refer to large tracts of land. They show that when territories came to be defined, it was often in terms of the tribal groups which had settled them. Society developed, but family loyalties remained vital. Safety lay in knowing that relatives would avenge one's death, and to neglect such vengeance meant undying shame. Already in Tacitus' day, however, honour might be satisfied by a *wergild*, a payment by the slayer to his victim's kin. Anglo-Saxon law codes list scales of *wergilds* in accordance with the victim's rank, and kings increasingly encouraged this non-violent type of retribution.

Tacitus also stresses the loyalty of the *Germani* to their lords. Sometimes they had hereditary kings, but in battle they were usually led by elected chiefs: 'It is a lifelong infamy and reproach to survive the chief and withdraw from the battle. To defend him, to protect him ... is the essence of their sworn allegiance.' Nine centuries later, in 991, an Anglo-Saxon army was defeated by Vikings at Maldon on the Essex coast. By then England was a civilized state, long since Christianized; yet the words which a contemporary poet ascribes to one of the defenders after his leader's death are a clear echo of Tacitus:

> 'I swear that from this spot not one foot's space
> Of ground shall I give up. I shall go onwards,
> In the fight avenge my friend and lord.
> My deeds shall give no warrant for words of blame
> To steadfast men on Stour, now he is stretched lifeless,
> —That I left the battlefield a lordless man,
> Turned from home. The irons shall take me,
> Point or edge.'

Clearly, loyalty to lord might sometimes conflict with loyalty to kin. In the interests of good order and their own authority, later kings tended to promote lordship: thus King Alfred's laws allow any man to 'fight on behalf of his born kinsman, if he is being wrongfully attacked, except against his lord, for that we do not allow'. But on both counts, Anglo-Saxon society always set great store by faithfulness and the keeping of oaths.

Their principal gods were those of later Norse mythology, Tiw, Woden, and Thor. They are remembered in the day-names Tuesday, Wednesday, and Thursday, as well as in a few placenames (Tuesley (Surrey), Wednesbury (Staffs.), Thursley (Surrey), etc.) which presumably indicate cult centres. Even when converted, the English named one of the main Church festivals after their old goddess Eostre. Shrines, like those of the *Germani*, were in remote places, in woods or on hills: a few place-names include the element *hearg* (shrine), as at Peperharrow (Surrey) and Harrow-on-the-Hill. Since later Church councils forbade the veneration of 'stones, wood, trees and wells', it can be presumed that such activities featured in pagan English cults. At least in its outward forms, this religion does not look so very different from that of the pagan Britons under Roman rule.

The narrative of events before *c*.600 does not amount to much. Plagued by the Picts and Scots, says Gildas, the British under the 'proud tyrant', Vortigern, imported the first Saxons to defend the east coast. Bede and other sources add that the Saxons were led by brothers named Hengist and Horsa, who founded the kingdom of Kent, and date their landing to about 450. Although this is rather too late, the tale is very consistent with the archaeological evidence: if Germanic mercenaries were settled under Roman rule, it is entirely likely that the successor states continued the same policy. Then, according to Gildas, the mercenaries rebelled and attacked their hosts; many years of inconclusive warfare followed, culminating in a major British victory, perhaps in *c*.500, at an unidentified place called *Mons Badonicus*. Meanwhile, the *Chronicle* notes the arrival of other chieftains on the south coast, the semi-legendary ancestors of later kings: Aelle in Sussex in 477, and Cerdic and Cynric in Wessex in 495.

One figure from these years who is familiar to everyone is, of course, Arthur. Unfortunately he has only the most shadowy claims to historical reality. The two or three possible fragments of genuine tradition were written down centuries later, and the legends which have gathered around his name are romantic inventions from the twelfth century onwards. We can only say that there seem to have been memories of a British war-leader called Arthur, who was associated with the battle of *Mons Badonicus* and subsequent campaigns. Possibly there was such a chieftain or over-king, the last man to unite the former Roman province before it collapsed finally into a patchwork of

British and Anglo-Saxon states. So general is our ignorance of major political events that there seems little point in speculating further.

Gildas says that the peace won at *Mons Badonicus* lasted until his own time, fifty years later, when there were five British kingdoms ruled by wicked 'tyrants'. How far their power still extended into the future English lands is a matter for conjecture, but the re-fortification of hilltop sites in the south-west suggests many years of inconclusive skirmishing. Through all this time, as excavated cemeteries prove, the invaders were pushing steadily further inland, up the Thames Valley, westwards from East Anglia, and northwards from Wessex. The *Chronicle* shows the Wessex Saxons advancing into Wiltshire in the 550s; capturing a large block of the South Midlands in 571; and winning a decisive battle at Dyrham (Glos.) which gave them Gloucester, Cirencester, and Bath in 577. Meanwhile, other English kingdoms were emerging from the shadows: the East Angles, the East Saxons, the Mercians, and the Northumbrian kingdoms of Bernicia and Deira. By the end of the century we are again on the firm ground of some reliable facts, and find the invaders in permanent control of half the island.

What had happened to the native peoples? Sixth-century Scotland was still mainly Pictish, though the settlements of Irish (the future 'Scots') on the west coast had created a settled kingdom, Dalriada. Centuries later, a king of Dalriada was to initiate the formation of a united Scotland. There were also three northern British kingdoms: Strathclyde, centred on Dumbarton, Rheged on the Solway Firth, and Elmet in the region of Leeds. Northumbrian designs on the Picts were ended by a major defeat in 685, and expansion here was mainly at the expense of the Britons. Strathclyde survived, but Rheged and Elmet were swallowed up by Northumbria during the late sixth and seventh centuries.

The main British enclave was, of course, Wales. Refugees from the east had doubtless swelled its population. Christianity survived, and with it some distinct traces of Roman culture. Scores if not hundreds of little monasteries were probably founded there during the sixth century, and charters from south-east Wales suggest the continuance of functioning Roman estate units. The kingdoms of Gwynedd, Dyfed, Powys, and Gwent existed by *c.*550, and some minor kingdoms by the end of the century. At least two of Gildas's tyrants ruled in Wales: Maglocunus (Maelgwn) of Gwynedd, 'first in evil, mightier than many both in power and malice', and Vortipor (Gwrthefyr) of Dyfed. Vortipor's monument still remains in a Dyfed churchyard—a reassurance that some substance underlies the rantings of Gildas:

Your head is already whitening, as you sit upon a throne that is full of guiles and stained from top to bottom with diverse murders and adulteries, bad son of a good king ... Vortipor, tyrant of the Demetae. The end of your life is gradually drawing near; why can you not be satisfied by such violent surges of sin, which you suck down like vintage wine—or rather allow yourself to be engulfed by them? Why, to crown your crimes, do you weigh down your wretched soul with a burden you cannot shrug off, the rape of a shameless daughter after the removal and honourable death of your own wife?

Cornwall, Devon, and Somerset formed the British kingdom of Dumnonia. Its king, according to Gildas, was as bad as the others: 'Constantine, tyrant whelp of the filthy lioness of Dumnonia.' The inhabitants were pushed back by the Anglo-Saxons during the seventh and eighth centuries, though Cornwall held out until 838. Thanks to this relatively late conquest, much survived. Excavation suggests that in some of the old cities, especially Exeter, Dorchester (Dorset), and Ilchester, life of a sort trickled on through the fifth and sixth centuries. Many major churches in these counties have Celtic origins: excavations at Wells in 1978–80 revealed a sequence of religious buildings from a late Roman mausoleum to the Anglo-Saxon cathedral. Here, as in Wales, smaller churches can often be traced back to a Celtic monastic enclosure (*llan*) or a cemetery around a martyr's grave (*merthyr*).

The hardest task is to estimate British survival in the regions which were firmly Anglo-Saxon by 600. From the facts that England in 1086 probably contained less than half its late Roman population, and that even this was after growth during the tenth and eleventh centuries, it is clear that depopulation in the fifth and sixth centuries was indeed drastic. Many fled westwards, or else to Brittany, and epidemic disease may have played its part. More generally, the Romano-Britons simply suffered a common fate of shattered societies; the decline in numbers is perhaps the clearest sign that their society *was* shattered. This is not to say that none remained: there are hints that the population contained substantial British elements, especially in the north and west. Sometimes (in the early Kentish laws, for instance) they appear as peasants or perhaps semi-servile estate labourers—which helps to explain how elements of Roman land organization may have passed into English society. Significantly, the English word *Wealh* ('Welshman', i.e. Briton) came to mean 'slave', making it hard to know whether the place-name Walton means 'the Britons' settlement' or 'the slaves' settlement'. However numerous, they were subservient: little of their culture passed to the Anglo-Saxons, and almost none of their language.

The early Anglo-Saxons were a non-urban people: their important places were important for hierarchical rather than economic reasons. But the view that they looked on the crumbling Roman towns with nothing but superstitious fear goes too far. The English knew what a *ceaster* was (the word is used with remarkable consistency), and often they knew its Roman name: *Mamucion* becomes *Mame-ceaster* (Manchester), *Venta* becomes *Ventan-ceaster* (Winchester), and so on. Towns occupied focal points in the road system, and their walls were strong. They were good places for chieftains to make their headquarters, and some towns may never quite have lost their local administrative functions. This does not, of course, amount to urban life: the Roman towns were not totally abandoned, but *as towns* they died.

Why was Roman Britain obliterated so much more completely than Roman Gaul? One reason is that the settlers were different: the Franks and Visigoths had come to know far more about Roman ways than the Angles and Saxons ever did. But it may also be true that the Britons themselves had changed greatly between the early fifth and mid-sixth centuries. The earliest Welsh poems show a society remarkably like that of the Saxons, dominated by the same loyalties and with the same emphasis on treasure, gift-giving, and the fellowship of warriors in their chieftain's hall. Even if no Saxon had ever set foot in Britain, it may be that its Roman civilization would have proved too fragile to last.

The Seventh Century

The first impression of early seventh-century England is that it was divided into large kingdoms: Kent, Sussex (the South Saxons), Wessex (the West Saxons), East Anglia, Essex (the East Saxons), Mercia (including the Middle Angles), and Northumbria (comprising Bernicia and Deira and, a little later, Lindsey). Reality was not quite so neat. Kingdoms were only gradually emerging from a state of flux: Middlesex, for instance, is probably the remains of a much larger Mid-Saxon territory dismembered before any surviving records could note it. There were also an unknown number of smaller peoples, lying between the big kingdoms or absorbed within them. Some, like the Hwicce of Worcestershire and the Magonsaete of the Welsh border, had their own kings who were gradually subordinated as the 'sub-kings' or 'aldermen' of greater rulers. There may have been many others: Surrey had a 'sub-king' named Frithuwold in the 670s, and it is quite possible that his ancestors had been rulers of an independent kingdom. There are also occasional hints of local separatism, and resentment against the bigger powers. Bede says that in 643 a monastery in Lindsey refused to receive the Northumbrian King Oswald's corpse, since although they knew he was a holy man 'he had

ENGLAND IN c.600

come from another province and had taken authority over them'. It is possible that in 600 English kings could be counted in dozens.

Even the big states experienced a shifting power balance. Bede and other sources mention a series of over-kings (*Bretwaldas* or *Brytenwaldas*), from various kingdoms but successively wielding authority over all or most of the Anglo-Saxon peoples. Whether or not the *Bretwalda*-ship was a formal office (which seems doubtful), it was certainly possible for an individual king to establish an extensive, if short-term, political dominance.

The first four in Bede's list, Aelle of Sussex, Ceawlin of Wessex, Æthelberht of Kent, and Raedwald of East Anglia, bring us to the 620s. We cannot say what their authority may have meant outside their own kingdoms, though we know that in 616 Raedwald took an army through Mercia, and defeated the Northumbrians on their own frontier. The fifth and sixth were both Northumbrian rulers, Edwin (616–32) and Oswald (633–42). These are Bede's heroes, his models of victorious Christian kingship. It is with them that we first get a clear idea of relations between the English kingdoms.

Northumbrian expansion westwards led Mercia to make common cause with the Welsh. In 632 Cadwallon, Christian British king of Gwynedd, and Penda, pagan Anglo-Saxon king of Mercia, won a short-lived victory over Northumbria, but the following year Oswald recovered power and Cadwallon was killed. The Welsh continued to support Penda, and in 642 Oswald was slain at Oswestry, campaigning far from home. This fact, and an incidental reference to his relations with the king of Wessex, show that Oswald's lordship and military activities extended far outside Northumbria. A group of early Welsh poems give the other side of the story from Bede's: his heroes are their aggressors. In the lament for Cynddylan, a nobleman from Powys who seems to have died in Penda's service, we glimpse the Northumbrians through British eyes:

> My brothers were slain at one stroke,
> Cynan, Cynddylan, Cynwraith,
> Defending Tren, ravaged town
>
> .   .   .   .   .   .
>
> More common was blood on the field's face
> Than ploughing of fallow
>
> .   .   .   .   .   .
>
> The hall of Cynddylan, dark is the roof,
> Since the Saxon cut down
> Powys's Cynddylan and Elfan . . .

In 655, Penda was defeated and killed by the Northumbrian Oswy, Bede's seventh over-king, who thereafter enjoyed great influence over the other kingdoms. None the less, the rising star was Mercia. The Mercian nobility soon expelled Oswy and chose Penda's son Wulfhere as their king. By the early 670s Wulfhere seems to have dominated the southern English kingdoms, and in 679 his successor won a victory at the Trent which finally ended Northumbrian expansionism. In the south, however, Mercian power was abruptly checked by Caedwalla of Wessex, who annexed Kent, Surrey, and Sussex during his short reign of 685–8. Caedwalla and his successor Ine built up a resilience of power in Wessex which was to determine the fate of England two centuries later.

In the world of seventh-century politics, then, it was possible to gain great power but hard to keep it for long. Why did kings rise and fall so quickly? One reason is that power and conquest depended on military forces; forces were attracted by gift-giving; gift-giving depended on wealth; and wealth in its turn was gained by power and conquest. Society was riddled with feuds, and the succession to kingdoms was fluid and uncertain; hence there were many royal and noble exiles from their own kin in search of generous and congenial lords. King Oswin of Deira, says Bede, 'was tall and handsome, pleasant of speech, courteous in manner, and bountiful to nobles and commons alike; so it came about that . . . noblemen from almost every kingdom flocked to serve him as retainers'. Such a system could hardly be stable: when a king grew sick, poor, or mean his retinue would collapse, and his heirs, if they survived at all, would become sub-kings or followers of a new lord.

What kingly magnificence could mean was brought to life, in 1939, by the discovery of a great royal burial at Sutton Hoo on the East Anglian coast. Since it seems to date from the 620s it was probably the tomb of King Raedwald, the fourth in Bede's list of over-kings. He was buried in a ship under a great mound, with his armour, weapons, and a mass of incomparable treasures. The gold and jewelled ornaments are perhaps the finest of their kind surviving in northern Europe, and no less remarkable is the range of countries from which items in the barrow came. An extraordinary ceremonial whetstone can scarcely be anything other than a sceptre. To judge from Sutton Hoo, poetic accounts of royal wealth contain no exaggeration: kingdoms were won and lost for treasures such as these.

From its beginnings, English society included a military aristocracy, probably with some kind of territorial base. But in the early centuries the king's followers or 'thegns' were tied less to their estates than to the king himself. They were expected to accompany him, to witness his public actions, to live in his hall, and if necessary to fight and die for him. Aristocratic life was strongly communal: the great hall as a place of good cheer, a haven in a dangerous world, is a powerful image in Anglo-Saxon writing. Nobody puts it better than Bede, in the famous words which he gives to a Northumbrian nobleman who is urging King Edwin to accept Christianity:

'This is how the present life of man on earth, King, appears to me in comparison with that time which is unknown to us. You are sitting feasting with your ealdormen and thegns in winter time; the fire is burning on the hearth in the middle of the hall and all inside is warm, while outside the wintry storms of rain and snow are raging; and a sparrow flies swiftly through the hall. It enters in at one door and quickly flies out through the other. For the few moments it is inside, the storm and wintry tempest cannot touch it, but after the briefest moment of calm, it flits from your sight, out of the wintry storm and into it again. So this life of man appears but for a moment; what follows or indeed what went before, we know not at all.'

The company in the royal or noble hall provided the audience for a literature which mirrored the age: heroic lays recited by professional bards. The surviving fragments include one major epic, *Beowulf*. As we have it, this is a relatively late and sophisticated work, perhaps written for a clerical audience. Yet it lays before us the heroic, essentially pagan world of the seventh-century aristocracy, transmuted by Christianity but not effaced. Its hero, Beowulf, is an exile who takes service with

Hrothgar, king of the Danes. A generous giver of treasure and splendid weapons, Hrothgar attracts to his court noble warriors who make him powerful. But the political world of the poem is violent and unstable: a king who loses support will quickly perish, and his kingdom with him. The ethos is one of loyalty and feud: 'It is better for everyone that he avenge his friend, rather than mourn him long . . . let he who can win glory before death.' Beowulf fights with monsters and dragons, inhabitants of a pre-Christian mental world. When he is killed, his followers lay him with rich treasures in a mound overlooking the sea, just as the East Angles had done for their king on the headland at Sutton Hoo:

> Then the warriors rode around the barrow
>
> .   .   .   .   .   .
>
> They praised his manhood and the prowess of his hands,
> They raised his name; it is right a man
> Should be lavish in honouring his lord and friend.
>
> .   .   .   .   .   .
>
> They said that he was of all the world's kings
> The gentlest of men, and the most gracious,
> The kindest to his people, the keenest for fame.

But there was more to early Anglo-Saxon society than warfare, savage loyalties, and ostentatious splendour. In some ways this was a surprisingly orderly world. The institutions which made the English state so exceptionally strong in the central Middle Ages have roots in the seventh century or even earlier: the efficiency of 'local government' was one important reason why new overlords could establish power so quickly. By the tenth century, English counties were divided for legal and administrative purposes into areas called 'hundreds'. In some at least of the early kingdoms, hundreds were formed out of larger but equally coherent districts, great blocks of fifty to a hundred square miles which apparently existed by the mid-seventh century. These have long been recognized in Kent, but recent research has detected them also in Northumbria, Mercia, Wessex, Sussex, and Surrey. The origin of this startlingly comprehensive system for dividing up the countryside is one of the great unsolved problems in early English history. Was it, as many believe, a Romano-Celtic survival? Was it created by one of the shadowy sixth-century *Bretwaldas*? Or did it develop spontaneously in the various kingdoms, reflecting common elements in the settlers' social background? Whatever the answer, it remains an oddly stable substratum in an unstable political world.

At the heart of each early district was a royal manor house or *tun*, run by a local official but visited by the king and his retinue at more or less frequent intervals. Each modern county contains several such sites, some given away by place-names such as Kingston, others less obvious. It was these 'central places', not towns or even villages, which were the main local foci of early and mid-Saxon society. The scattered inhabitants of the district looked for law and government to the king's great hall with its surrounding buildings. Here too they paid their dues and other public burdens in accordance with a complex system of assessment. Land was reckoned in 'hides', each notionally the area needed to support a free peasant cultivator and his family, and often an actual farm unit. Obligations, it seems, were assessed by the hide, and hides were grouped into multiples of twenty or more which owed obligations of a specialized kind. The king's deputy at the centre might thus receive renders of grain from some groups of hides, of calves or foals from others, and of honey, mead, or lesser commodities from others again.

Thus the early administrative districts were organized for exploitation as well as for jurisdiction. A system of economically specialized zones suited the underdeveloped countryside, with its sharp geographical contrasts and large areas of uncleared common pasture. So it is not surprising that when mid-Saxon kings granted away blocks of land, these early 'manors' often preserved the internal structure of the districts from which they were formed. Hence the 'multiple estate', the federation of distinct 'vills' or townships linked to one manorial centre, which was still prominent in many parts of England in the twelfth and thirteenth centuries. Some historians have recently argued that this type of organization (which certainly resembles that of early Wales) was of Celtic origin. Some continuity in rural organization is quite likely, but perhaps only in a sense so broad that it ceases to mean much. It was growth and social change, not conquest, which eventually made the 'multiple estate' obsolete. Granted that the British peasants were not all driven out, and that their way of life was probably not so very different from the invaders', it would be surprising if a pattern which suited existing resources had *not* continued.

This pattern also suited a peasant population which was dispersed, unstructured, and relatively small. The most prominent figure in the early sources is the free peasant farmer or *ceorl* (modern English 'churl', but without its derogatory sense), typically cultivating one hide of land. This does not mean that all seventh- and eighth-century farmers were so 'free' that they had no lord save the king. After the Conversion kings granted blocks of land to churches, as they had probably done to lay followers (at least on a temporary basis) from earlier still. The origin of the 'manor' as a private unit of jurisdiction and revenue is obscure, but some historians place it near the very beginnings of English society. The medieval division of estates into 'demesne' (exploited directly by the lord) and peasant land is recorded by the late seventh century, and much of the manpower on demesnes was provided by slaves. But in the early stages it seems likely that lesser lords, like kings, drew revenue from smallholders without greatly altering their way of life or farming methods. There is no evidence for the hierarchical, thoroughly dependent groups of tenants who existed by the tenth century; nor for the organized 'village communities' which seem so closely linked to strong lordship in the twelfth and thirteenth centuries. Archaeology suggests that most farmsteads in mid-Saxon England were either isolated or in little clusters, and even the nucleated settlements lack any sign of the orderly streets, greens, and plot-boundaries familiar from later village topography. It now seems likely that medieval common-field systems, with holdings intermixed in scattered strips, result from several centuries of evolution. In seventh-century England the integrated 'village community' was still in the future.

Into this very traditional society of kings, warriors, and farmers there came in 597 an alien influence—the Christian Church. The conversion of the English was initiated by Pope Gregory the Great, who according to tradition had seen English youths in Rome and pronounced them 'not Angles but angels'. Gregory knew that King Æthelberht of Kent had a Christian Frankish queen; thus it was to Kent that he sent the first mission, headed by a Roman monk named Augustine. Æthelberht, hesitant at first, soon converted, and Augustine founded a monastery at Canterbury. Misjudging the survival of Romano-British life, Gregory had planned archbishoprics based in London and York, but political realities were acknowledged in 601 when Augustine was enthroned as first Archbishop of Canterbury. Initially, success seemed rapid. In 604 a see was founded at Rochester; the East Saxons were converted, and a cathedral dedicated to St. Paul was built for them in London. Meanwhile several monasteries were built in Kent, their churches closely modelled on Roman prototypes.

But the skin-deep conversion of a king and his household was a shaky foundation at best. The East Saxons soon apostatized and expelled their bishop. Despite his baptism King Raedwald of the East Angles remained ambivalent, for Bede reports that he maintained simultaneously a church and a pagan shrine. In Northumbria the story is similar. King Edwin received the Roman missionary Paulinus, and was baptized with his thegns in 627. But on his defeat and death only five years later, his successors apostatized and Paulinus had to flee. The Church had speedily gained a foothold in the English courts; but a broader basis was needed if it was to rise above the ebb and flow of political fortunes.

Surprisingly, it was not the Gregorian mission which was most successful in this respect but the primitive, isolated Celtic Church. The Christians of Wales and Cornwall probably had some influence on the English, but it was scarcely very significant. Augustine, who seems to have been a rather proud, humourless man, offended the Welsh bishops and no co-operation resulted. The mission which achieved so much among the northern English came rather from Ireland to Scotland, and thence to Northumbria.

Thanks to St. Patrick and his followers, Ireland was largely Christian by the early sixth century. Monasteries multiplied, so much so that the whole Irish Church came to be organized along monastic lines. 'Provinces' were based on monasteries and were ruled by abbots; bishops performed their normal spiritual functions, but they lacked formal dioceses and were under the abbots' authority. Hence the typical Irish missionary was the wandering bishop owing obedience to a community at home. The Irish houses were to reach a level of wealth and sophistication far surpassing their counterparts in Wales, and already in the sixth and seventh centuries they were sending missionaries to Gaul, Germany, Scotland, and England. One named Columba went to Scotland, converted the northern Picts (the southern Picts were already Christian), and in c.563 founded a monastery on the island of Iona. When the Christian King Oswald won control of Northumbria in 633 it was naturally to Iona that he turned for a missionary, for his exile had been spent among the Irish of western Scotland.

The simple, wandering life of the Irish bishops and monks brought them in touch with the people at large. Aidan, Oswald's bishop, had the qualities needed to convert Northumbria permanently. After building a monastery on the island of Lindisfarne, he set up a church in each royal vill from which to preach to the countryside around. Bede says that he always travelled on foot, thus meeting passers-by on equal terms. Several monasteries were founded, and soon the Northumbrian Church was strong enough to branch out into other kingdoms.

Penda of Mercia remained pagan but allowed a mission from Lindisfarne to work in his realm, and his son Peada was baptized in 653. The over-kingship of Oswald and then of Oswy helped the Northumbrian Church to spread. In 635 Oswald's influence caused Cynegils of Wessex to accept baptism from a missionary named Birinus, who became first bishop of the West Saxons. Thanks to Oswy, the East Saxons re-converted and received a Northumbrian bishop named Cedd, who had been trained in the Irish Church. By 660 only the men of Sussex and the Isle of Wight remained pagan, and soon they too were converted.

The zeal of the Irish missionaries had achieved much; in the long run the authority of the Roman Church was bound to count for more. If Pope Gregory's aims were to be realized, the Celtic Church in English kingdoms had to accept the discipline of Rome. The main sticking-point was an issue which now seems absurdly trivial—on what day should Easter be celebrated? In their long isolation, the Celts had adopted computations which differed from those used at Rome. When the two Churches came into contact, the results could be inconvenient: at the Northumbrian court the Irish-trained King Oswy sometimes celebrated Easter while his Kentish-trained wife was still observing Lent. The question itself had a deep religious and symbolic importance; for the future of the English Church, resolving it was more important still. At the Synod of Whitby (664), King Oswy of Northumbria came down in favour of the Roman party, and the few Celtic die-hards returned to Iona. This was the turning-point: the Church through all the English kingdoms could now become a united and uniting force under one primate.

None the less, the Church was beset with problems in the 660s. Organization was haphazard; there were far too few bishops, and some were invalidly consecrated. Others died in a plague in 664, which also made the East Saxons apostatize again. But in 669 the pope sent a new archbishop, a native of Asia Minor named Theodore. This surprising candidate (only chosen when several others had refused) was just what was needed: a firm administrator. During his thirty-year reign, he rationalized the diocesan structure, which had been fluid everywhere and perhaps almost absent from kingdoms converted by the monastically-organized Irish. Bishops with invalid orders were disciplined, and dubious authorities either ratified or annulled: all acts of the Welsh bishops, for instance, were declared void. A synod held at Hertford in 672 established the first basic canons for Church government.

Most churchmen accepted Theodore's rulings with good grace, but not the formidable Wilfrid, bishop of Ripon and then of York. Wilfrid was firmly orthodox and had championed the Roman Easter at Whitby, but he resented any threat to his power in the Northumbrian Church. His stormy relations with Theodore and successive kings involved two expulsions, two appeals to Rome, exile, and imprisonment. Meanwhile he managed to preach to the Frisians, convert Sussex, and found monasteries in Mercia. With his retinue and huge wealth, Wilfrid seems an extraordinary mixture of saint and secular nobleman. Only a young and essentially aristocratic Church could have produced such a figure.

Theodore's reign was a golden age for monasteries. On the one hand, the great Celtic houses such as Lindisfarne and Whitby were increasingly influenced by Roman ways, though the old values lived on: in St. Cuthbert the solitude and austere devotion of the Irish missionaries was combined with Roman attitudes to monastic life and discipline. On the other hand, many new houses founded in these years would be counted for centuries among the greatest in Britain. In some ways the most important of these were Wearmouth and Jarrow, founded by Benedict Biscop, a Northumbrian nobleman turned monk. Biscop had been five times to Rome, and his twin monasteries brought to Northumbria the culture of the Mediterranean Church. Their most celebrated member, Bede himself, describes how Biscop had a church built by Gaulish masons 'in the Roman manner which he always loved', filled it with rich pictures and furnishings, and built up a great library from Continental sources.

Impressive though these achievements were, there was also a need to provide some permanent basis for the Church's work in the countryside: it is hard to believe that the conversion of the peasantry had hitherto been more than superficial. Many will find it surprising that here, too, the first stages were achieved by monastic or quasi-monastic bodies. With hindsight it seems obvious that missionary work and pastoral care are activities for priests, not monks. But in the seventh and eighth centuries this line was not quite so firmly drawn, even outside the Celtic Church. The English word *mynster* (monastery) was used for institutions ranging from true Benedictine houses to small, loose-knit communities of priests. Rules varied greatly (Biscop composed his own for Jarrow), and so did standards; we really have very little idea of what life was like in all but the greatest houses. But it is becoming clear that by 750 England contained hundreds of small 'minsters' with genuine and important pastoral functions, serving what may be called the first English parochial system.

The 'old minsters', as they came to be called, were older than the mass of ordinary local churches, and served much larger areas. Most of the sources are late, and show them as near-obsolete establishments with only residual authority. Hence we know little of their pastoral work, except that it existed. It appears that the collegiate priests, or deputies in the case of strict monks, travelled about within a defined 'parish' preaching to local communities. The 'parishioners' of the minster owed it their tithes, and were obliged to bring to it their children for baptism and their dead for burial. So complex a system could not have evolved so quickly without royal patronage. Paulinus and Aidan preached from their kings' vills (see p. 76), and it is no surprise to find many minster churches sited at royal *tuns* (see p. 75). Tithe-duty was probably based on existing tax assessments, and some kings may have founded several minsters as an act of policy, as Oswy of Northumbria seems to have done in 655. Kings had an organized system of local government; so, therefore, did the Church. Though eventually smothered by the thousands of little churches which sprang up within them, minster 'parishes' moulded the whole future development of the Church in the English countryside.

If kings helped the Church to grow, the Church also enhanced the status of kings. The grandsons of pagan war-leaders were coming to see themselves as God's appointed deputies; a few generations later, the crowning of a new king became something very like an episcopal consecration. With Christianity, too, came literacy: kings could revise and formulate tribal custom to resemble the legislation of the civilized world. Æthelberht of Kent, says Bede, made his laws 'according to the custom of the Romans'. Æthelberht's code, and the later seventh-century codes from Kent and Wessex, suggest a mixture of local tradition with borrowings from the Continent. Whatever their practical usefulness (which is doubtful), the kings who made them clearly wanted to seem sophisticated: lawgivers in the classical mould. As the kingdoms were opened more and more to influences from Rome and Gaul, the nature of kingship changed. It was becoming important for rulers to uphold justice and direct the internal affairs of their kingdoms, not merely to win battles. Even the seventh-century codes, with their long lists of fines and penalties, suggest an impressive range of royal authority.

Also with the first English churches, we start to glimpse the first English towns. Possibly sixth-century rulers had set up headquarters in the Roman towns and forts; certainly seventh- and eighth-century rulers favoured them as sites for cathedrals and minsters. Canterbury, York, Winchester, and Worcester cathedrals were all built within Roman defences, and in 635 the first bishop of Wessex was given the Roman fort at Dorchester-on-Thames, called by Bede a *civitas*, to found his see. Royal halls and churches built on abandoned ruins are not in themselves towns. None the less, the most highly-organized communities of the age were surely the cathedrals and minsters;

craftsmen, tradesmen, servants, and beggars all gravitated to their doors. It is no coincidence that the first hints of reawakening urban life are associated with major churches, both in Roman towns and on the more numerous sites with no pre-English origins. The first archaeological evidence for Anglo-Saxon settlement in Canterbury is slightly later than the building of Augustine's cathedral there. At Northampton, recent excavations have shown that the nucleus of the town was an eighth-century minster church and hall, with associated buildings. A late ninth-century translation of Bede's term *urbana loca* is not, as we would expect, 'towns', but 'minster-places'. Scores of English towns began as minsters with lay settlements converging on their gates.

The Mercian Supremacy

England in the early eighth century was a more sophisticated place than it had been in the early seventh. A united English kingdom was still far away, but the English were now starting to become aware of themselves as an ethnic and cultural unity. Bede may have felt this more keenly than anyone: it is easy to forget how significant is the very title of his greatest work, *The Ecclesiastical History of the English People*. It was because he saw the common destiny of his race fulfilled in the united English Church that he could think of an 'English people'. But are there any signs that secular government was also becoming more comprehensive? This is a hard question to answer, not least because there are more sources. On the one hand, institutions and concepts which show the strong side of eighth-century kingship may not be new, but merely recorded for the first time. On the other hand, the dynastic turmoils which show its weak side may not be new either: it is possible that Bede and his contemporaries glossed over such matters. This at least can be said: as *Bretwaldas* on the old pattern the eighth-century Mercian kings were as mighty as their forerunners; and they lived in a world of greater literacy and legality, of firmer-entrenched rights, which made their power more stable and more capable of development.

Æthelbald of Mercia (716–57) inherited much of the influence won by Wulfhere. Written charters recording royal grants were now appearing in some quantity, so we can see how kings liked to style themselves. Æthelbald's titles are impressive, but perhaps not wholly new. 'King not only of the Mercians but of all the provinces called by the general name Southern English', as one charter calls him, echoes Bede's statement that the early over-kings 'held sway over all the provinces south of the River Humber'. The claim can be supported to the extent that charters show him influencing Kentish affairs and controlling London. But Wessex remained independent, as did Northumbria under Bede's patron King Ceolwulf: Mercian supremacy was never to go north of the Humber.

Æthelbald's successor Offa (757–96) was the most powerful English king before Alfred. His position once secured (which took some years), his conduct in all the kingdoms except Northumbria and Wessex seems to have been more that of a direct ruler than a remote overlord. Earlier kings had suppressed small royal dynasties, but Offa suppressed great ones. He had full control over Kent (with a brief interlude in the late 770s), and treated its king as his servant. Once he annulled a grant by King Egbert of Kent, 'saying that it was wrong that his minister should have presumed to give land ... without his witness'. After an unsuccessful coup against Offa's successor in 798, the ancient Kentish dynasty was extinguished for ever. The last king of Sussex appears as one of Offa's *duces*; in Surrey, which had been West Saxon territory, we find Offa confirming a grant by a Mercian noble. In East Anglia (though here the dynasty reappeared later), the *Chronicle* notes laconically for 794: 'In this year Offa, king of Mercia, ordered [King] Æthelberht's head to be struck off.' In Wessex, royal power and tradition were stronger: the kingdom only recognized Mercian protection between 786 and 802, and even then the lordship seems to have been of a much vaguer kind than in Kent.

Offa is the first ruler whose charters use the simple, unqualified title 'king of the English'. His status is emphasized by a famous letter to him from the great Frankish king, Charlemagne. Charlemagne addresses him as an equal, 'his dearest brother', and speaks of 'the various episcopal sees of your kingdom and Æthelred's' as though Offa of Mercia and Æthelred of Northumbria were the only kings in England. The Frankish connection is important (though possibly too much has been made of this one document: there had always been plenty of contact between Gaul and the southern English). Offa would certainly have liked to be thought another Charlemagne, and whatever the reality of royal power, its status certainly rose in line with developments abroad. In 787 Offa had his son Egfrith made king of the Mercians by a solemn consecration which Northumbria copied nine years later. The semi-sacred character of kingship was becoming stronger.

This did not make dynasties more stable. Succession was uncertain: long after Offa, kings would still be 'chosen' from the royal stock. Any vaguely eligible candidate with forces behind him could aim at the throne, and Mercia, Wessex, and Northumbria were all torn by dynastic feuds during the eighth century. In his efforts to secure the succession, Offa seems to have been as ruthless towards relatives as he was towards neighbours. When his son Egfrith died shortly after Offa himself, the Northumbrian scholar Alcuin saw it as a judgement: 'The vengeance for the blood shed by the father has now reached the son; for you know very well how much blood his father shed to secure the kingdom on his son.'

Much of this shows Offa in a savage light, but some important institutions did start to take shape under the Mercian kings. The Church was now firmly established with lands and privileges. Its assemblies were solemn affairs, recorded in writing. Æthelbald and Offa were often involved in Church councils and sometimes presided over them; their thegns and ministers witnessed decisions. The way Church business was conducted can hardly have failed to heighten the sense of precedent and legality. Though the context is ecclesiastical, such assemblies must have helped to transform the *ad hoc* band of warriors around a seventh-century king into the formal 'Witan' or grand council which we find in late Saxon England.

The concept of 'bookland' (land for which a written charter gave legal title) was now well established. Most eighth-century charters, at least the surviving ones, are grants to churches, but they reflect a society in which rights in the land and local interests were winning ground against traditional values. The eighth-century aristocracy begin to seem a little less like warriors, a little more like country gentlemen, and evidence starts to appear for family houses and family churches. Little is known of the houses, though one has been excavated at Goltho, Lincolnshire: a mid-ninth-century defended enclosure containing a hall, kitchen, chamber, and outbuildings. For the churches there is more evidence: hereditary 'private' minsters, controlled by families of noble patrons, often figure in eighth-century sources. All this is equally true to the mightiest lord of all. Earlier kings had had their royal vills, but Offa seems to have tried to make his residence at Tamworth a kind of national headquarters or 'capital'. Near Tamworth was the Mercian cathedral of Lichfield, which Offa managed to have raised for several years into an archbishopric. If this was partly for political reasons, there was much to be said for a metropolitan church near the 'metropolis' of Offa's kingdom.

The duty of landowners to help in the building of bridges and fortifications first appears in a document of 749, and is usually stipulated in later grants of land. This is significant in an age which produced massive public works of at least two kinds: one long-famous, the other only recently understood. The first is, of course, Offa's Dyke, so called by an ancient and probably correct tradition. Recent excavations suggest that this enormous earthwork was a continuous barrier between England and Wales, running from sea to sea. Offa is known to have raided into Wales, but the Dyke must be a defensive rather than an offensive work, built to stop a Welsh counter-

attack when plans for conquest had been abandoned. But the fact that it exists at all is proof of the huge resources which Offa commanded.

The charter references to 'fortress-work' imply fortified strongholds rather than dykes. It is well known that Alfred and his heirs developed a network of large communal fortresses or *burhs* to protect Wessex against the Vikings. Archaeology has recently begun to suggest that some *burhs* are a century or more older, and may have been founded to defend Mercia in its years of greatness. In most cases (for instance Bedford, where Offa is said to have been buried), the evidence is still only topographical, and therefore inconclusive. But at Hereford, excavation has revealed an eighth-century defended circuit pre-dating later Saxon enlargements, and less conclusive evidence for defences of Offa's period has been found at Tamworth. Several of the late ninth-century Wessex *burhs* may also have earlier origins; some, such as Wareham (Dorset), Dorchester (Dorset), and Oxford, are certainly on sites which were important in the eighth century or before.

We have seen two factors in the emergence of towns: churches and fortresses. The third, in the long run the biggest, is trade. Offa lived in an age when foreign and internal trade were both expanding. The clearest sign is the appearance of a systematic coinage. Until *c.*600, only foreign gold coins had circulated in England. The crude silver coins minted by seventh- and eighth-century kings were unreliable, and usually of localized circulation. A new Frankish currency of silver pennies was the model for a better coinage, and an East Anglian king seems to have used it slightly before Offa. But when Offa's beautiful pennies did appear, they quickly drove out older issues and gained a wider circulation than any currency since Roman times. Perhaps the most interesting point is that Offa's coins have been found not only in large hoards, but also in small, scattered groups. Evidently, they were used for small-scale transactions at a local level: money was becoming of general importance in the English economy.

A dispute with Offa in 789 caused Charlemagne to close Frankish ports to English merchants. Hence it seems that English merchants normally used such ports: Charlemagne's realm and Offa's were part of a growing world of international commerce. Trading centres were appearing throughout northern Europe. Excavations on the huge settlements of Hedeby in Denmark and Birke in Sweden have produced finds suggesting that in the eighth century England and the Viking lands belonged to the same international trading community. In England, commercial settlements such as these were often linked to existing royal and ecclesiastical centres, and their names often include the element *-wic* (from Latin *vicus*). *Hamwih* was the precursor of modern Southampton. It lay at the junction of the Test and Itchen near a royal vill called Hampton, and its name labels it as the *Ham-wic* associated with the *Ham-tun*. Here excavation has disclosed a settlement of at least 30 hectares, probably first occupied in about the 720s, with artefacts suggesting wide European contacts. Others were probably Ipswich (*Gips-wic*), a major pottery-producing centre, Sandwich, and Fordwich. Roman towns started to regain economic as well as hierarchical importance. A commercial suburb developed at York (*Eofor-wic*), where Frisian merchants are recorded; at Canterbury excavation has revealed eighth-century houses, and a market is mentioned in 786. Most important was London, which Bede could describe in *c.*730 as 'an *emporium* of many peoples coming by land and sea'. This commercial zone has proved hard to find, though it now seems that the Roman and medieval waterfronts at Billingsgate include a mid-Saxon clay bank. Wherever it lay, it must have been large and important: *Lunden-wic* is mentioned in the late seventh century, and eighth-century sources refer to tolls and tax-gatherers at its port.

The eighth century was a rather unsettled time for the English Church. Lay foundation and patronage of ministers had brought its own problems. Hereditary interest was not necessarily a bad thing: in the hands of a responsible family, a monastery could expect both security and prosperity. But not all proprietors were responsible; while some minsters, if we can believe Bede, were simply 'fronts' for tax evasion. Bede was not alone in worrying about lax standards. Æthelbald, Offa, and his successor Cenwulf (796–821) participated in a series of much-needed reforming synods. Monks were forbidden to live like lay nobles; drunkenness and secular songs in monasteries were condemned. In 786, Offa held the only council in the Anglo-Saxon period to be attended by papal legates. But if the growth of Church government enhanced royal dignity, it also raised the pretensions of bishops. Relations between Church and State were not always easy, especially with a king like Æthelbald who seems to have combined monastic reform with robbing minsters and seducing nuns. Dealings between the king and the Archbishop of Canterbury tended to be complicated by the strong anti-Mercian feeling in Kent. Archbishop Jaenbert was outraged when Offa raised Lichfield to an archiepiscopal see, and the scheme was abandoned after the king's death on the grounds that it had been prompted by enmity towards the people of Kent.

On the positive side, the English Church did produce one outstanding scholar, Alcuin. A product of the cathedral school at York, he was a leading figure in Charlemagne's court and took a central part in Charlemagne's great revival of classical learning and education. It is significant, especially in the context of Charlemagne's letter to Offa, that the dominant intellectual of late eighth-century Europe was an Englishman. But it must be remembered that Alcuin, like Bede before him, was a Northumbrian: we know very little about Mercian culture. Probably this simply means that much has been lost. Mercia had no Bede to record its achievements, and its greatest monasteries were sacked by the Vikings. Fragments of decorative art, such as the sculptures in the minster of Breedon-on-the-Hill, suggest sumptuous physical surroundings. A noble monument to the age of Æthelbald and Offa is the great minster church of Brixworth, Northamptonshire. It is a sign of how much we do *not* know that this monastery fails to appear in any early document, unless it is the lost *Clofesho* where the Mercian synods were held.

The most impressive fact about the eighth-century Church is that the English were now taking Christianity to their original homelands on the Continent. The mission began, oddly enough, through St. Wilfrid's quarrel with Archbishop Theodore. Setting out in 678 to state his case at Rome, Wilfrid travelled through pagan Frisia and spent a year preaching. The Frisians were well known to the English from their merchants, and Wilfrid opened the way to more ambitious missionary work. A group of Northumbrians landed in Frisia in 690. Among them was Willibrord, who took the lead and was consecrated Archbishop of Frisia in 695. He established his cathedral at Utrecht, and the organized Church of Frankish Frisia developed quickly. Willibrord's work was supplemented by a West Saxon mission led by St. Boniface. Between his arrival in 718 and his murder by pagans in 754, Boniface preached among the Frisians, Germans, and Franks, setting up a see at Maine. As well as converting pagan areas Boniface had great influence on the Frankish Church as a whole, regulating it and bringing it under papal guidance. Through his career he relied on books, recruits, and advice from England, and there survives a large correspondence with friends at home. Much of the work which transformed the stagnant Frankish Church into the expanding Church of the Carolingian revival was done by English men and women.

The Viking Invasions and the Rise of the House of Wessex

Mercian power did not long outlast Offa. His successor, King Cenwulf, kept hold of Kent and Sussex and even gained some new territory from the northern Welsh, but Wessex slipped from his grasp in 802. A new dynasty of overlords was about to appear, this time West Saxon. In 825 Egbert of Wessex won a decisive victory near Swindon, expelled a Mercian under-king from Kent, and annexed Kent, Essex, Surrey, and Sussex. Four years later, Mercia itself fell to Egbert, and even Northumbria acknowledged his lordship. The reversal is spectacular, and shows that Offa's dynasty had done little to stabilize English politics. Nor could Egbert: by his death in 839 Mercia was independent once again. The old interplay of dynasties seemed to be continuing much as ever. But under the year 789 the *Anglo-Saxon Chronicle* contains an ominous entry: the first breath of a storm that was to sweep away all rivals to the house of Wessex, and with them some of the best achievements of English civilization:

In this year Beorhtric [king of Wessex] took to wife Eadburh, daughter of King Offa. And in his days came first three ships of Norwegians from Horthaland: and then the reeve rode thither and tried to compel them to go to the royal manor, for he did not know what they were: and then they slew him. These were the first ships of the Danes to come to England.

This Viking landing was a minor affair, though there are other references soon afterwards to 'sea-borne pagans' attacking the south coast. More serious, and incomparably more distressing, were raids in the north, for they involved the successive plundering of Lindisfarne (793), Jarrow (794), and Iona (795). England had been safe from foreign attacks for two centuries; the reaction to the sudden desecration of three of its most holy places is easily imagined. These were, however, isolated incidents, and it was a generation before the Viking nuisance became a major threat. But a big raid on Kent in 835 opened three decades in which attacks came almost yearly, and which ended with the arrival of a full-scale invading army.

The dramatic expansion of the Norwegians and Danes is a European phenomenon, of which the raids on England and Ireland were only one part. Two races were involved (the word *Viking*, 'pirate', was coined by their victims and refers equally to both), and several motives. They were far from being total barbarians, and by the 840s they had been heavily involved in trade for some generations. It was, indeed, this trade which opened up regular contact with the nations to the west and south. Population grew, and it became hard to find a reasonable living at home. Many adventurers must have heard stories of the fertile lands with monasteries full of easy plunder, and it is surprising rather than otherwise that the early raids were not followed up more quickly. The fall of the Danish royal dynasty in 854 left a power vacuum, with no strong king who could unite warriors and prevent them from dispersing on foreign exploits.

These factors help to explain why raiders descended in such numbers on European countries from the 850s onwards, and why casual plundering gave way to a policy of conquest and settlement. There seem to have been two main routes: one around the north of Scotland to the Western Isles and so southwards, the other to the east and south coasts of England and to Gaul. Hence the raids and settlements in Ireland, Scotland, Wales, and Cornwall were mainly Norwegian, while those in the English and Frankish lands were mainly Danish.

In 865 the Danish 'Great Army', led by Halfdan and Ivarr the Boneless, landed in East Anglia. After a few months' stay it turned northwards into Northumbria, which happened to be split by a dynastic dispute, and captured York in 867. Both the rival kings perished, and the Danes set up their own nominee to rule Northumbria as a client state. The army then advanced into Mercia, but on meeting opposition it withdrew to York without an open fight, and in 869 descended again on East Anglia. The inhabitants were defeated in battle, and their king Edmund (soon to be venerated as St. Edmund the Martyr) became the victim of a ritual murder. Within three years, the once-great kingdoms of Northumbria and East Anglia had ceased to exist.

In 870 the Danish army camped at Reading and prepared to invade Wessex. But here the opposition was better organized. After Egbert's death the West Saxons were ruled by his son Æthelwulf, an unambitious but capable man. Æthelwulf's main achievement seems to have been to avoid the kind of family feuding which had ruined other dynasties: his four sons succeeded peacefully in order of age. When the Vikings attacked, the third son, Æthelred, was on the throne; the name of his brother and heir, Alfred, was to become the greatest in Anglo-Saxon history.

It was a combined force under Æthelred and Alfred which met the Danes on the Berkshire Downs and inflicted their first serious defeat. But the English success was short-lived. The Danes withdrew to Reading, but almost immediately advanced again and defeated Æthelred and Alfred near Basingstoke. In April 871 a new Danish army landed. Invasion of Wessex seemed imminent, and its defenders had nowhere to turn for help. In the midst of this crisis Æthelred died, and his brother became king of the West Saxons.

Alfred the Great (871–99) is known to everyone as the king who saved England against seemingly hopeless odds. This is not quite how contemporaries would have seen it. In political terms at least, 'England' still did not mean very much. The first writer known to use *Angelcynn* (literally '[the land of] the English folk') was Alfred himself, and *Englaland* does not appear for another century. It was not a foregone conclusion that the other kingdoms would accept West Saxon lordship, or even prefer it to the Danes. They might well have chosen kings of their own, and there was always a danger that English rivals, exiles, or disaffected groups would enlist Viking support. The destruction of the other dynasties did not automatically make Alfred king of all the English; he and his heirs achieved this through a mixture of military success, tactful diplomacy, and good luck.

The reign started badly, and after a year of minor defeats Alfred had to buy the Danes off. They left Wessex alone for five years, during which they invaded Mercia, expelled King Burgred, and replaced him with their own nominee: a third ancient kingdom had gone for good. The Great Army now split into two halves. One, led by Halfdan, turned north and began dividing up Yorkshire for permanent settlement. The other, led by Guthrum, Oscytel, and Anund, turned south, and in 875–6 launched another attack on Wessex. At first their success was limited; in 877 they withdrew again to partition out Mercia, and another group split off to colonize Lincolnshire, Nottinghamshire, Derbyshire, and Leicestershire.

Thus it was a much-reduced force which attacked Wessex for the third time in 878. However, a surprise attack on Chippenham gave them the upper hand; much of Wiltshire and Hampshire submitted, and Alfred was driven back to a refuge at Athelney in the Somerset marshes. The position seemed hopeless, but Alfred bided his time in his fortress and gathered troops. Early in May, says the near-contemporary writer of the *Chronicle*, 'he rode to *Ecgbrihtesstan* [Egbert's Stone] . . . and came to meet him there all the men of Somerset and Wiltshire and part of Hampshire . . . and they rejoiced to see him. And one day later he went from those camps to Iley Oak, and one day later to Edington; and there he fought against the entire host, and put it to flight.'

The victory was sudden but decisive. The Danish leader Guthrum accepted baptism with several of his captains, and the two kings settled peace terms. These recognized the Danish occupation of much of England as a *fait accompli*. The frontier ran roughly north-westwards from London to Chester; Guthrum was to withdraw with his troops behind this line, where he was to be recognized as king of an independent kingdom. By the autumn of 880 the Danes had left Wessex and begun the systematic settlement of East Anglia.

This was not the end of the conflict. In 886 Alfred captured London, apparently after defeating a Danish garrison. In 893 a big Danish army landed in the Thames estuary and raided through England during the next three years, but this time it made little impression on Wessex. Alfred had been busy, both in securing the safety of his own kingdom and in consolidating his lordship over the other territory west and south of the Danish frontier. For the first task, he seems to have improved both the army and the navy. Kings had long been entitled to levies of troops raised in accordance with the land assessment in hides. Alfred's reorganization, by which only half of the army was to be on service at any one time, foreshadows the later 'select fyrd' or militia: it must have produced a smaller but more efficient host. An obvious way of combating sea-borne raiders was with more ships, and Alfred is said to have built vessels much bigger than the Vikings', carrying sixty oars or more.

The most important element in his programme (certainly the one which saved Wessex from further inland raids) makes Alfred the first English town planner. By the late 880s Wessex was covered with a network of public strongholds, several of which have a regular grid of streets and can only be described as planned fortified towns. A document called the *Burghal Hidage* lists thirty of these *burhs*, with three more which may be later additions. Perhaps the most impressive case is Winchester, where a new grid ignoring the Roman streets was laid out within the Roman walls. The same linearity can be seen at Oxford, Chichester, Wareham, and others. Planning was remarkably systematic, and it seems that the surveyors used a standard 66-foot measure for setting out the streets. The larger *burhs* were more than just fortresses, and soon acquired an important role in the local rural economy. Manning the defences was the responsibility of neighbouring landowners, who were able in return to use the defended area for their own purposes. Often they built 'town houses' in the *burh* to store their produce for marketing: Domesday Book records several links between urban tenements and rural manors. Traders and craftsmen followed, and the strongholds of the late ninth century became the thriving towns of the tenth. Defence happened to coincide with the needs of a growing economy; thus Alfred has his unexpected but permanent memorial in the road systems of several modern towns.

One important reason for Alfred's long-term success was the tact with which he treated his neighbours. In Mercia especially,

it was dangerous to wound local pride. Alfred left affairs there
in the hands of the old royal council, headed by a Mercian
nobleman named Æthelred who became his son-in-law, and
when he took London in 886 he immediately handed it over to
Mercian control. Thus treated, Æthelred was staunchly loyal to
the Crown, and after Alfred's death he and his wife Æthelflaed
led Mercian offensives against the Danes. If Alfred was more
truly 'king of the English' than anyone before him, it was not
just through military strength or because no rivals remained:
people genuinely wanted him because they knew that he and
his family were just and considerate rulers.

But there remained the problem of the Danes and the damage
they had done. Some of it was irreparable: whatever happened
now, the world of Bede and Offa had gone for ever. The size of
the Danish Great Army may be disputed, but it is impossible to
deny the evidence of three kingdoms destroyed, dioceses dis-
rupted, innumerable monasteries plundered, charters and other
documents almost completely lost for much of eastern England.
The ruin of monasteries was perhaps the most serious, for the
great houses had been the main repositories of learning and
culture, while the small ones were still mainly responsible for
pastoral care in the countryside.

In the Danelaw (as the area behind Guthrum's frontier came
to be known) the Danish soldiers quickly established a society
of their own. Yorkshire, Lincolnshire, Leicestershire, and to a
lesser extent East Anglia are full of place-names ending in *-by*,
-thorp, and other Scandinavian elements. This impact is startling: it shows both that the army was very large, and that it
distributed itself widely over the countryside. Even when the
Danelaw was Christianized and brought under English rule it
retained striking peculiarities, with its own systems of manorial
organization, land measurement, law, and social differentiation.
Tenth-century kings had the problem of reconciling the claims
of a united kingdom with customs very different from those of
the English.

England badly needed a revival of literacy and learning, and to this Alfred devoted his last ten years. Like Charlemagne, he carried out his programme of education through a circle of court intellectuals. In some ways his own contribution to this project is the most remarkable of Alfred's achievements. He was the only English king before Henry VIII who wrote books. Lamenting the destruction of manuscripts and the decay of scholarship, he learnt Latin and translated works into English for his subjects' benefit. Among the many translations which his circle produced (and which include, significantly, Bede's *Ecclesiastical History*), three are probably Alfred's own work. It is also believed that the *Anglo-Saxon Chronicle*, as we now have it, may have been first compiled at Alfred's court. For priests, a good Latin education became once again necessary for high office. It is hard to know how well Alfred's Renaissance succeeded, but it must have provided more literate priests and a more learned laity: good foundations for the monastic reform of two generations later. Alfred was lucky that future events caused so many of his various schemes to bear fruit. Even allowing for this, he remains the outstanding figure of early English history.

The reigns of Edward the Elder (899–924), Athelstan (924–39), and Edmund (939–46) were dominated by the reconquest of the Danelaw. This half-century was the formative period for national kingship. Dynastic feuds were avoided, partly through Alfred's careful provision for the succession and partly through some lucky chances. In 902 a dangerous split was averted when Edward's cousin, who had sought Danish help to win the crown, was killed in battle. Athelstan succeeded smoothly in 924 because he was both the rightful heir to Wessex and had been educated in his Mercian aunt's household. By the mid-century there was no serious possibility that Mercia, still less any other kingdom, could revert to an older dynasty. The royal house of Wessex was the royal house of England.

The campaigns of Edward's reign were mainly directed by the king himself in partnership with his sister Æthelflaed, 'the Lady of the Mercians'. The English offensive began when a

Danish raid into Mercia was defeated in 910. Over the next eight years, Edward pushed into the Danelaw while his sister kept the Danes busy on their Mercian frontier. Æthelflaed was now threatened from two directions, for Norwegian Vikings from Ireland had begun attacking the west coast. Her main achievement was to build a series of new Mercian *burhs*: on the east frontier against the Danes, on the west frontier against the Welsh, and in the north-west to block Norwegian raids on Tamworth from the Dee and Mersey. In 917 Æthelflaed took Derby, giving Edward a chance to invade East Anglia while the enemy was occupied. By 918 all the southern Danelaw had fallen to Edward, though isolated Danish armies were holding out in Stamford, Leicester, Nottingham, and Lincoln. Leicester submitted to Æthelflaed, but her death soon afterwards forced Edward to halt the campaign while he secured Mercia. Returning swiftly, he took Stamford, Nottingham, and Lincoln, and by the end of 920 the English frontier was fixed at the Humber.

Meanwhile, Edward was forming links with his other non-English neighbours. In 918 he received the 'submissions' of the Welsh kings of Gwynedd and Dyfed. In 923, says the *Chronicle*, 'the king of Scots and the whole Scottish nation accepted him as father and lord: so also did Raegnald and the sons of Eadwulf and all the inhabitants of Northumbria, both English and Danish, Norwegians and others; together with the king of the Strathclyde Welsh and all his subjects'. These were the first in a series of such 'submissions', culminating in an extraordinary spectacle in 973 when eight 'British kings' swore fealty to Edward's grandson Edgar and rowed him on the River Dee.

It must be emphasized that these were personal submissions to the kings to whom they were made: they involved the acceptance of lordship and protection, not the permanent surrender of independence. In fact, Scotland and Wales were both advancing towards their own internal unity. In *c.*850 Kenneth Mac Alpin, king of the Scots, had annexed the Pictish kingdom, and over the next two centuries Scotland developed under Scottish (as against Pictish) rule. In Wales, politics were transformed by the sudden expansion of Gwynedd from the late ninth century onwards, leaving only Dyfed of the smaller kingdoms. The Anglo-Saxons never conquered Wales or Scotland, and in each a native power had emerged dominant by 1066. None the less, Wales was much influenced both by England and by the Vikings.

Among the many groups competing for land in tenth-century Britain was a new one—the Norwegians from Ireland. They had no fondness for the Danes, and their main object was to gain control of the northern Danelaw. In 918 a force led by Raegnald attacked Scotland, based itself in Northumbria, and the following year took York, where Raegnald established himself as king. The Norse kingdom was to last, with interruptions, for thirty-five years, during which trade grew and the twin Norse cities of York and Dublin expanded fast. Excavation at York has revealed streets of timber houses and shops, laid out by the Danes and redeveloped by Raegnald's followers. During the reigns of Athelstan and Edmund, the enemies of the English were the Norwegians more than the Danes.

In 920 Edmund had accepted Raegnald's fealty and thus acknowledged his status. But when a new Norse king tried to seize his inheritance in 926, Athelstan attacked and captured York, destroyed its defences, and received the submission of the kings of Scotland and Strathclyde. Six years later, relations between Athelstan and the Scots broke down. Fearing invasion, the various rivals of the English made common cause. But in 937 the English army under Athelstan defeated a combined force of Norse, Scots, and Strathclyde Welsh. Athelstan was now at the height of his power, king of the English and Danes and in some sense overlord of the British. He was respected by foreign powers, and formed marriage alliances with the French and German royal families. His charters show the Welsh princes regularly attending his court; Hywel Dda, king of Dyfed in Athelstan's time, imitated English silver pennies and issued laws modelled on English codes.

But much still depended on the individual king. Soon after

Athelstan's death in 939, a Norse army returned under Olaf Guthfrithson. The new king Edmund was forced to recognize Olaf as king of York and its dependent territories. Olaf died in 941, and during the next four years Edmund recovered the northern Danelaw and ravaged Strathclyde. Especially interesting here is a contemporary poem in which Edmund features as liberator of the Danes from their Norse oppressors: the great-grandsons of Alfred's enemies could identify with the English Crown rather than with their fellow Scandinavians. But in 947, the year after Edmund's death, York fell yet again to a Norse king, Eric Bloodaxe. The next six years saw a confused struggle between Eric, the new English king, Eadred, and a Norwegian rival named Olaf Sihtricson. In 954 Eadred invaded Northumbria, this time for good, and the last king of York was driven out and killed.

From nearly fifty years of complex warfare the house of Wessex had emerged triumphant. The tranquil reign of Edgar (959–75) proves that more had been created than mere military power. Edgar was not a conqueror: one historian has written that 'his part in history was to maintain the peace established in England by earlier kings'. But this was no mean achievement: the kingdom was young, and it is with Edgar that the main developments in late Saxon kingship come into focus.

From Athelstan onwards, kings made laws more frequently and went into more detail. They cover a wide range of subjects—peace-keeping, the suppression of thieves, the hierarchy of churches, the conduct of merchants and markets, to name only a few. The emphasis is on unity: Edgar's codes make allowance for local custom, especially in the Danelaw, but insist that 'the secular law shall stand in each folk as can best be established'. By the early eleventh century the trying of most serious crimes was reserved to the Crown, and there was a concept of a national peace which it was the king's duty and right to maintain. Royal authority was spread wider, and went deeper, than in any other tenth-century European country of comparable size.

Laws and charters were issued at meetings of the 'Witan' or royal council. Its development can be traced by means of the witness lists attached to charters. In the tenth century it was much bigger and probably more formal than the councils of earlier kings, and included numerous men described as 'ministers' or thegns. Some nineteenth-century historians tried too hard to see the Witan as a 'proto-parliament': it was in no sense a democratic body, nor did it impose 'constitutional' restraints on the king. But it was important. In the Witan new kings were chosen, solemn public arts were ratified, and business was discussed. It was composed of nobles, bishops, and many men of influence in their own localities. From Athelstan's reign onwards, the enlarged Witan was an established institution and a force to be reckoned with.

The king's will operated through a much-improved system of local government. During the tenth century, the regional anomalies of England were progressively reduced to a single framework of 'shires'. Some had existed for a century or more, and many were based on still older boundaries. But it was essentially under Edgar that the English counties stabilized in the form which lasted until 1974, exactly a thousand years later. The shires were entrusted to a group of leading magnates, the aldermen. In ninth-century Wessex there had been an alderman for each shire, but by a gradual process, which seems to start under Athelstan, the number of aldermen fell and their status rose. By Edgar's reign the alderman was becoming less like a local official, and more like his successor the eleventh-century earl. But he still remained in regular touch with the government of the shires under his care.

For legal and administrative purposes the shires were broken down into subdivisions, called 'hundreds' in most counties, and 'wapentakes' in the northern Danelaw. Each hundred had its own court for settling local business, and communal obligations to provide troops and oarsmen came to be assessed by the hundred. Even this was not the bottom of the ladder: for law enforcement the population was organized into groups of ten

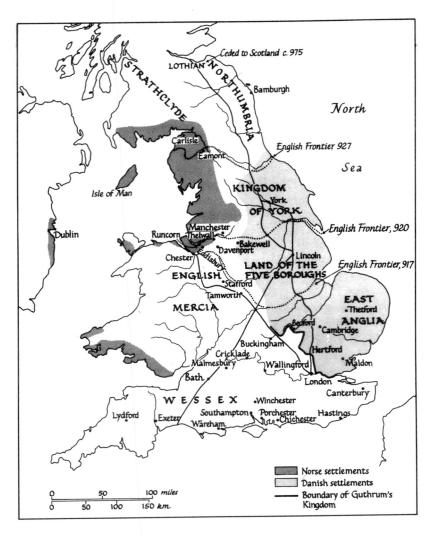

ENGLAND IN THE TENTH CENTURY

mutually-responsible households or 'tithings'. The weight of royal government reached the individual peasant through a structure of remarkable complexity. How much was new in the tenth century is hard to say. The principle of the hundred appears in earlier law codes, and it seems likely that late Saxon hundreds were often or usually based on older territories. But the system was rationalized and improved by Alfred's successors, and under Edgar it emerges clearly in its developed form.

Another mark of royal strength was the coinage. Even before Alfred, the three coin-issuing authorities (the kings of Wessex and Mercia and the Archbishop of Canterbury) had agreed on a standard currency of silver pennies. Decrees issued by Athelstan between 924 and 939 order that 'one coinage shall run throughout the land'. He and his heirs managed to maintain uniformity remarkably well, and all coins were minted by strictly-controlled moneyers in the *burhs*. In *c*.973 Edgar designed a new coinage of pennies, which remained the basis of the English currency until long after the Conquest. The excellence of the coins shows a degree of control which was, once again, unique in contemporary Europe.

Edgar's main personal achievement was his encouragement of monastic reform. True Benedictine monasticism seems to have been almost dead in early tenth-century England. Several great and innumerable small minsters had been destroyed by the Danes, while those which survived had tended more and more towards the loose, secular life-style that Bede had long ago deplored. Groups of minster priests lived in separate houses with their wives and children; in their everyday existence they came closer to cathedral canons than to monks. A successful reconstruction of the English Church would need models for the new monasticism, and money to build the new monasteries. The first was provided by the great European reform movement, of which the English reform was essentially a part; the second was provided by Edgar and his nobility. The prime movers were three great churchmen, St. Dunstan, St. Æthelwold, and St. Oswold.

The monastic reform in England began in the early 940s, and under royal patronage: Glastonbury, given to Dunstan by King Edmund, and Abingdon, given to Æthelwold by King Eadred, were the first of the 'new' houses. But Edmund and Eadred were both lukewarm, while the next king, Eadwig, had a personal grudge against Dunstan. This had productive consequences, for Dunstan was exiled abroad and gained a wide knowledge of European monasticism. Times changed with Edgar's accession in 959: Dunstan became Archbishop of Canterbury, and Æthelwold bishop of Winchester. Oswold, the youngest of the three, had spent some time in the French monastery of Fleury. Dunstan persuaded Edgar to give him the bishopric of Worcester, and soon afterwards Oswold built a monastery at Westbury-on-Trym. Over the next half-century some fifty houses were founded or refounded under the influence of Glastonbury, Abingdon, and Westbury.

The monks in the new monasteries followed a way of life based on the rule of St. Benedict, with elaborations in ritual and daily routine in line with Continental practice. In c.970 the various traditions were combined in the *Regularis Concordia*, one rule for all the English houses to follow. Edgar's part was crucial: he gave the weight of his authority to the movement, and all the new monasteries were under his direct patronage. The expulsion of secular priests from the old minsters to make way for monks, which first happened at Winchester in 964, would have been difficult without royal backing. Edgar gave generously, and expected others to do likewise: by the 970s there are signs that the drain on aristocratic funds was becoming resented. None the less, to found a monastery was once again a socially prestigious act.

The new houses were wealthy, respected, and endowed with treasures and fine buildings. Literary sources hint at the richness of English art under Edgar. A number of the magnificent illuminated books survive, but only fragments of the gold, enamel, and ivory ornaments, and almost none of the major buildings. Fate has been unkind to late Anglo-Saxon architecture, for all the greatest churches were rebuilt after the Conquest. As enlarged in the tenth century, the Old Minster at Winchester was 250 feet long, with side-chapels, elaborate western towers, and carved and painted friezes. But it must be stressed that this spiritual and material regeneration touched only a fraction (probably under 10 per cent) of the old communities: the others continued in their former ways. Thus at the Norman Conquest the Benedictine houses co-existed with an unknown number of small secular minsters, relics of the pre-Viking English Church.

If the new monasticism owed much to Europe, it was distinctively English in its relations with the state and society at large. By 1000 most English bishops were monks, and both bishops and abbots deliberated with lay magnates in the Witan. Great churchmen were among the most valued advisers of the last Anglo-Saxon kings. Equally, Church reform added lustre to a king who, perhaps more than any of his predecessors, set store by the sacred character of his office. Edgar's coronation in 973 was postponed until he reached thirty, the minimum canonical age for ordination to the priesthood. The climax of the ceremony was not the crowning, but the anointing with holy oil which conferred near-priestly status and set the king above human judgement. As the homilist Ælfric of Eynsham put it, 'no man can make himself king, but the people have the free will to choose him to be king who is most pleasing to them. But once he has been consecrated king he has power over the people, and they may not shake his yoke from their necks.' The frontispiece of the Winchester New Minster foundation charter shows Edgar as he wanted to be seen: crowned, standing between two saints, and offering his gift to the heavenly king through whom earthly kings rule.

Æthelred and Cnut: the Decline of the English Monarchy

The next two reigns would show that there were still great limitations on the national monarchy. A new king could not count on loyalty before he had won it, as was shown when Edgar died in 975 leaving two sons under age. The elder, Edward, became unpopular, and many nobles preferred his brother Æthelred. Edward was crowned, but four years later he was murdered at Corfe. There can be little doubt that Æthelred's supporters were responsible, and the murder was a fitting start for an unhappy reign. Æthelred 'the Unready' (979–1016) has always had a bad press (though his famous nickname has lost its original meaning, which involved the pun *Æthelræd Unræd*, 'Noble-Counsel No-Counsel'). Probably he did lack the qualities which were still so important for kingship: the knack of putting trust in the right places and commanding trust in others. On the other hand, law and justice continued to develop in his reign under the guidance of the learned Archbishop Wulfstan. If it had not been for a new problem—the return of the Vikings—the English state might have held together as well as it had done under Edgar.

The new raiders were even more dangerous than their ninth-century ancestors. By the 970s the Danish king, Harold Bluetooth, who had gained control of both Denmark and Norway, was creating a formidable army of highly-trained professional soldiers. In 988 Harold was deposed by his son Swein, who maintained his father's army and built large fortresses to house military communities. One of these has been excavated at Trelleborg in Denmark. It consists of a large circular earthwork enclosing groups of great boat-shaped halls, all planned with mathematical precision. Both Trelleborg and the Danish sagas suggest a degree of co-ordination and discipline which the English army would have found it hard to match.

The attacks began within a year or two of Æthelred's accession. At first they were on a fairly small scale, but in 991 a large Danish force defeated Alderman Byrhtnoth and the Essex militia at Maldon, and had to be bought off with a large payment. The pattern was repeated after heavy raids in 994, 997, and 1002. It is for these payments that Æthelred's reign is now so notorious. Huge numbers of his pennies have been found in

Scandinavia, and several Swedish tombstones commemorate mercenaries who went to England and enriched themselves with tribute. In the 990s, as in 1066, England's wealth was also its danger.

How was Æthelred to cope? One measure was to prevent the harbouring of Vikings by his neighbours, and for geographical reasons the young duchy of Normandy was the most important of these. The Normans were only a few generations away from their own Viking ancestors, and had sometimes opened their ports to raiders returning from England. But in 991 King Æthelred and Duke Richard made a treaty against aiding each other's enemies, and ten years later Æthelred married the duke's daughter. So began the fateful association of Normandy and England.

Hitherto the king's internal policy does not seem to have been very different from that of his predecessors. He inherited a powerful, well-established aristocracy, and his early charters show him building up support with grants of land just as Eadwig and Edgar had done. But from 1002 the Viking threat became rapidly more severe, and exposed a basic weakness in royal power. The king's lands, and probably his activities generally, were still heavily concentrated in Wessex. The resources with which he could buy support in the north and east were very limited—and these were just the areas where support most needed to be bought. They still had separatist tendencies, and contained many people who remembered their Danish origins. Æthelred's later charters show a shift of patronage into the Midlands and eastern England, and new men of non-Wessex origin become prominent. The king was struggling to hold England united and in a state of defence. His ineptitudes may have made the task harder, but nobody would have found it easy.

The strain on the government was demonstrated when, in 1002, Æthelred and his council ordered a massacre of all the Danes living in England. This extraordinary command cannot have been fully enforced—in some areas the population was largely Danish—but it hints at something approaching national hysteria. We know that, when the Danes in Oxford took refuge in St. Frideswide's minster church, the citizens burnt it down. This massacre almost certainly prompted the Danish invasion of the following year, led by King Swein himself. Swein sacked Norwich, but his East Anglian campaign involved heavy losses and in 1005 he withdrew to Denmark. Next year he returned, led his army through Berkshire, Wiltshire, and Hampshire, and once again had to be bought off with a large payment. In the ensuing respite the government built a new fleet, but early in 1009 eighty of the ships were burnt through the treason of an English captain. On the heels of this misfortune, another Danish army landed, led by Thorkill the Tall and Hemming. In 1010 they burnt Oxford, and then moved to East Anglia from which they raided into Kent the following year. The campaign ended unexpectedly in 1012 when Thorkill changed sides, disgusted by his own army's brutal murder of Archbishop Ælfheah. This brought forty-five ships into Æthelred's service; the rest of the army left England.

The feebleness of England's defences was now clear to all, and when Swein returned in 1013 it was with the intention of conquest. Disillusioned with Æthelred's government, the men of the Danelaw welcomed a Danish king and accepted Swein almost immediately. By the end of the year he had taken Oxford, Winchester, and London, and Æthelred had fled to exile in Normandy. In February 1014 Swein died; his son Harold succeeded to his Scandinavian empire, but the army in England accepted Harold's younger brother Cnut as their king. Meanwhile Æthelred had returned, and by spring he was fielding an expedition against the Danes. Caught unprepared, Cnut withdrew to Denmark. In 1015 he was back with a bigger force, to find that Æthelred's son Edmund Ironside had taken control of the northern Danelaw in defiance of his father. During the next few months Cnut recovered Northumbria and then moved towards London. But before the Danish forces arrived Æthelred was dead and Edmund had been proclaimed king. Even in

Wessex, however, many men accepted Cnut's lordship without a struggle. Edmund rallied his forces, and for a little while it seemed that the Danes might still be driven back. But in the autumn of 1016 Cnut won a decisive battle at Ashingdon in Essex. The treaty which followed left Edmund with only Wessex, and when he died shortly afterwards Cnut became king of all England.

King Cnut (1016–35) had to deal with problems which were not dissimilar to those which faced King William fifty years later. Like William, Cnut set out to rule not as a conqueror but as a rightful English king. He married Æthelred's widow, and acted ruthlessly to secure the throne: several leading English were killed, including Æthelred's eldest surviving son. Once secure, Cnut adopted with enthusiasm the traditional attributes of civilized kingship. He issued laws and founded monasteries; in the words of a chronicler of the next century, he changed himself 'from a wild man into a most Christian king'. Yet he was still a Dane, and on his brother's death in 1019 he inherited a great northern empire of which England was only part. During the 1020s he became more and more involved in Danish affairs. The breadth of Cnut's involvements is the main reason for his changes in England, which were relatively few, but in the end damaging.

Naturally he had many followers eager for rewards. There was no full-scale replacement of the English landowning class such as occurred after 1066, but a good many Danes joined the aristocracy. An alien and therefore rather insecure king, Cnut kept a regiment of household troops or 'housecarls' who were a considerable burden on the country. After thirty years of paying to keep the Danes away, landowners now had to pay to support a Danish standing army.

Cnut also had to make English government function during his long absences abroad. In 1017 he divided the kingdom into four earldoms—Northumbria, East Anglia, Mercia, and Wessex. This ran obvious risks of reviving local separatist feeling, especially since the Northumbrian and East Anglian earls were both Danes. By the end of the reign the most important figures were Siward earl of Northumbria, Leofric earl of Mercia (whose wife was Lady Godiva of Coventry fame), and Godwin earl of Wessex. Godwin's origins are obscure, but by the 1030s he and his family were the wealthiest and most powerful laymen below the king. Cnut's earldoms are largely responsible for the power politics which dominate the last thirty years of Anglo-Saxon history.

The End of the Anglo-Saxon Kingdom

When Cnut died in 1035 there were several possible successors. The Wessex dynasty was represented by Æthelred's younger sons Edward and Alfred, now at the Norman court, and by Edmund Ironside's son who was exiled in Hungary. Cnut had two sons by two wives: Harold, by Ælfgyfu of Northampton, and Harthacnut, by Emma the widow of Æthelred. Cnut had wanted Harthacnut to succeed to his whole empire. But while Harthacnut delayed in Denmark the Witan appointed Harold as regent (despite the opposition of both Emma and Godwin), and in 1037 made him king. The previous year, the English prince Alfred had unwisely visited England and died of injuries inflicted at Godwin's instigation. Harthacnut was recalled after Harold's death in 1040, but when he died two years later the Danish royal line ended. Almost everyone now wanted to restore the ancient dynasty of Wessex. Æthelred's son Edward had been living for a year at the English court, and in 1042 he was elected king.

Edward 'the Confessor' (1042–66) was destined to be venerated as the principal English royal saint. His recent biographer, scrutinising the reality behind the pious legend, writes that 'he was not a man of great distinction. But neither was he a holy imbecile. He was, like many of his rank and time, a mediocrity.' Whatever his strengths and weaknesses, he inherited the strongest government in eleventh-century Europe. The reason for this strength lay partly in institutions which were centuries old, partly in the very disruptions of the last sixty years.

Local government had developed since Edgar's day. On the one hand, the great earldoms consolidated under Cnut had given huge territorial power to a few men. An insecure king now had to face the threat of over-mighty subjects. On the other hand, an invaluable new official had appeared to carry out royal policy in the localities. During Æthelred's reign one of the king's local bailiffs ('reeves') in each shire had come to be known as the 'shire-reeve' or sheriff. He was the king's chief executive agent in the shire, and gradually assumed more and more of the alderman's functions. The sheriff was responsible for collecting royal revenues and the profits of justice, but he also belonged to the growing community of local thegns. In the shire court he could announce the king's will to the gentry of the shire, take a big part in day-to-day business, and add the weight of royal authority to action against oppressive magnates. The shire court and the sheriff are among the most important Anglo-Saxon legacies to later medieval government.

A highly efficient tax system had evolved as a direct result of England's weakness under Æthelred. The huge sums paid to the Danes in the 990s had to be raised from the country. The 'Danegeld', as it came to be called, was based on the ancient method of assessing land in hides, and was raised at a fixed rate of so much per hide. Between 1012 and 1051 it was levied yearly by the successive kings, though now for maintaining their standing armies. The complex system of assessment developed for this purpose is the basis of the later Domesday Book, and it is an extraordinary tribute to the early eleventh-century English bureaucracy that the Norman kings continued to raise Danegeld for nearly a century after the Conquest.

This period also saw a new type of official document: the royal writ. Writs were possibly issued by Æthelred and certainly by Cnut, but the earliest which now survive as originals are from Edward's reign. In its initial form, the writ was a brief notification to the shire-earl and the sheriff or bishop that a grant of land had been made and should be witnessed in the shire court. A typical example reads:

Edward the king greets Harold the earl and Tofi his sheriff and all his thegns in Somerset in friendly fashion. And I make known that Alfred has sold to Giso the bishop the land of Lutton peacefully and quietly: he did this in my presence at Parret, and in the presence of Edith my wife, Harold the earl and many others who were there present with us. We also wish that the same bishop shall hold that land with all its appurtenances which the bishop possesses with sac and soc as freely as any of his predecessors as bishops ever did anything. And if anything be taken away from it unjustly we ask that it may be restored. Nor shall it be done otherwise.

This combined efficiency with a new means of authentication: a pendent wax seal, stamped from a die kept in the king's household. As title-deeds, writs provided useful supplements to the old formal charters, which were unwieldy and easily forged. They also provided a means for the king to make his will known quickly and clearly in the shires. The Conqueror soon adapted the writ for issuing orders, and all the more important types of post-Conquest royal document are descended from it.

When ordering a taxation or issuing a writ, the king would have consulted his secretariat. Edward the Confessor, like kings since Alfred at the latest, had a clerical staff of priests, headed by a chief clerk whose office developed into that of the medieval chancellor. One of their duties was to keep records: from the late Anglo-Saxon period comes evidence of very detailed surveys recording land-tenure, numbers of hides, and tax obligations. Some remarks by Bede suggest that even the seventh-century Northumbrian kings had enough precise information to grant land in exact numbers of hides; while from the eighth century a document called the *Tribal Hidage* lists the names and hidages of the peoples, provinces, and tribes dependent on Mercia. So we can be confident that ninth- and tenth-century kings had fiscal records of some kind, though how detailed is impossible to say. By Edward the Confessor's reign, the royal secretariat possessed rolls which listed the hidages of shires and hundreds, the amount of royal land they contained, and perhaps even the names, owners, and values of individual manors. We know this not from the documents themselves (though a few fragments survive), but from Domesday Book. The great survey of 1086 could scarcely have been compiled so quickly and so thoroughly if the commissioners had not had access to earlier lists. The loss of the pre-Conquest public records is tragic, but the mere knowledge that they existed says much for the quality of Edward's administration.

If English government changed greatly between the reigns of Alfred and Edward, so too did English society. The mid-ninth to mid-eleventh centuries saw rapid growth in the population and economy. Before Domesday Book there are no statistics, but written, archaeological, and topographical evidence gives some strong hints that many aspects of later English society crystallized in these years. Not surprisingly, more people meant bigger towns. By the Conquest there were English towns in a sense that we would understand today: large concentrations of people with markets and tradesmen, groups of craftsmen in specialized quarters, guilds and regulations, numerous churches, and in some cases rapidly expanding suburbs. The late Saxon law codes recognize trading centres or 'ports' (not necessarily coastal) and large boroughs, rated according to the number of moneyers they were allowed to contain. The towns included most of the *burhs* and many minster centres, but they were not confined to places of ancient importance. We cannot even guess at the number of local markets, but a good many which first appear in the thirteenth century may be older than they seem.

The countryside was also changing, though it is hard to trace the changes clearly. Topographical studies suggest a process of settlement nucleation in the more populous areas, with the inhabitants of scattered farms clustering into villages. At the same time, agriculture was becoming more complex and more integrated, so that by 1066 many parts of England had 'common fields', farmed by peasants with intermingled holdings, and therefore probably with corporately-agreed cropping patterns. The early development of field systems is now a controversial subject, but it is in the tenth century that we can first detect the basic contrast between the open-field zone of Midland England and the surrounding 'wood-pasture' areas. Much remains uncertain about the relationship between changes in settlement form, agriculture, and land-holding, but it seems that the process went through several stages and continued well beyond the Conquest. There are also suggestions that sometimes these were not spontaneous developments, but rearrangements planned from above. Peasant society was becoming more stratified and cohesive, and lords were making greater demands on their tenants.

One reason is that there were more manors and more manorial lords. Except in retarded areas, most of the old 'multiple estates' had fragmented by the eleventh century into units corresponding in size to modern rural parishes. Population grew, cultivation expanded, and the components of the old 'extensive' systems became self-contained entities. Many more charters survive from the tenth century than from the eighth and ninth together; most of them grant smaller units of land, and the proportion in favour of laymen is higher. The class of small thegns had broadened into a rural squirearchy, and Domesday Book shows that in 1066 England contained hundreds of manorial lords.

This is the context in which most parish churches were founded. Just as kings and bishops had built minsters in the seventh and eighth centuries, so thegns built manorial churches in the tenth and eleventh. There were *some* private churches from a relatively early date (Bede mentions a bishop consecrating one in the 690s), but both documents and archaeology suggest that the majority were founded after 900, perhaps even after 950. Pastoral organization must have been chaotic: the minster parishes were slowly decaying, and more and more of the manors within them were acquiring rival churches of their own, served by manorial priests. Eleventh-century churches (both before and after the Conquest) were in effect 'owned' by their lords, and their functions were determined on tenurial rather than pastoral lines: the church's function was to serve the needs of the lord, his household, and tenants. We can scarcely speak of anything so formal as a 'parochial system', though the raw materials were there: probably more than half the parish churches existing in 1700 were founded before 1066.

So the familiar landmarks of rural England—villages, manor houses, churches—took shape mainly in the late Saxon period. For Archbishop Wulfstan, writing in *c.*1010, the last two were normal marks of thegnhood: 'If a *ceorl* prospered so that he possessed fully five hides of land of his own, a church and a kitchen, a bell and a fortress-gate, a seat and special office in the king's hall, he was worthy thereafter to be called a thegn.' The 'fortress-gate' in this famous passage leads to a question which has become needlessly controversial: were there castles in pre-Conquest England? One writer, equating private castles with feudalism and convinced that late Saxon England was non-feudal, argues that it contained no fortresses beyond the communal *burhs*. But if a strongly-fortified manor house counts as a castle, the existence of castles says little about a society except that it included a land-based aristocracy of some status. In fact excavation now proves that fortified houses *did* exist, and complex manorial buildings surrounded by banks and ditches of *c.*1000–20 have been found at Sulgrave, Northamptonshire, and Goltho, Lincolnshire. These sites show that ordinary late Saxon thegns' residences could be as imposing as most manor houses of the twelfth and early thirteenth centuries.

Warfare was becoming more professional, and equipment consequently more expensive. By the end of the tenth century, a system of military service had developed in which every five hides was responsible for providing and equipping one man for the *fyrd* (militia). This acknowledged that the average farmer could not reasonably be expected to kit himself out from his own resources, and by implication raised the status of the fighting man. Five hides, according to Wulfstan, was a thegn's minimum estate, and armour and weapons had become another mark of thegnhood. The fully-armed late Saxon warrior was something more than a *ceorl* turned soldier.

By Æthelred's reign the monastic reform was running out of steam. Burton Abbey in Staffordshire (1004) and Eynsham Abbey in Oxfordshire (1005) were the last great foundations, and the general political disruption and draining of resources soon put a stop to large-scale patronage and building. Edward's piety did, however, produce one building project, the most ambitious that England had ever seen. In about 1050 he began to rebuild the old minster church at Westminster on a scale worthy of the English monarchy. Architecture in England was stagnant, but in Normandy its development during the last forty years had been spectacular: the finest buildings of Edgar's day would have looked unimpressive beside the abbey churches of Bernay and Caen. So for Westminster Abbey Edward naturally looked to Norman architects, though his church as eventually built was magnificent and innovative even by their standards, and probably owed something to English decorative traditions. It is somewhat ironic that the last great monument of the house of Wessex was mainly a product of Norman culture.

The final years of Anglo-Saxon history are dominated by Godwin's family and the problem of the succession. Edward had married Godwin's daughter, but by the early 1050s it had become clear that he would never produce an heir. Edward, son of Edmund Ironside, returned from Hungary with his infant son in 1057 but died almost immediately. The young prince Edgar was the legitimate heir, but nobody can have viewed with much enthusiasm the prospect of a child on the throne. The Norwegian king, Magnus, and after him his son Harold Hardrada, saw themselves as the heirs to Cnut's empire, including England. Neither candidate is likely to have appealed much to King Edward: his eyes, if they were turned anywhere, were turned across the Channel. The duchy of Normandy, where he had lived in exile for twenty-five years, had developed fast in strength and internal organization. In 1035 Duke Robert had been succeeded by his bastard son William, then a boy of seven. We will never know for certain if Edward promised his throne to William, but we can say that this is exactly the course which we might expect of him.

Edward had never forgiven Godwin for his brother's murder, and the tension between them came to a head in 1051. One of Edward's Norman friends became involved in a brawl at Dover, and several men were killed. Edward ordered Godwin, as earl of Wessex, to sack Dover in retribution. Godwin refused and raised troops against the king, who summoned the Mercian and Northumbrian earls with their full forces. Conflict was avoided; as a contemporary put it, 'some of them considered it would be great folly if they joined battle, because wellnigh all the noblest in England were present in those two companies, and they were convinced they would be leaving the country open to the invasion of our enemies'. Godwin's support crumbled, and he and his family went into exile. Over the next year Edward increased the Norman element at court, but in 1052 Godwin returned with a large fleet and the king was obliged to be more compliant. The Norman archbishop fled home, and several of his fellow countrymen were banished at Godwin's request.

Godwin now enjoyed virtually supreme power, but in 1053 he died. His successor in the earldom of Wessex was his son Harold, destined to be the last Anglo-Saxon king. When Earl Siward of Northumbria died two years later, his earldom went to Harold's brother Tostig. Thanks to the activities of King Gruffydd of Gwynedd, the standing of Godwin's sons soon rose yet higher. Gruffydd, who had recently made himself supreme in Wales, allied with the exiled heir to the Mercian earldom and launched a series of attacks into English territory, in the course of which Hereford was sacked and burnt. The combined forces of Harold and Tostig drove Gruffydd back into

Wales, and in 1063 caused his downfall and death. With this success behind him, Harold was the outstanding figure in England. Despite his lack of royal ancestry, he seemed an obvious candidate for the throne.

But in 1064, or perhaps early in 1065, Harold visited Duke William in Normandy. He went, say the Norman sources, as Edward's ambassador, to swear an oath confirming an earlier promise of the English crown. It is possible, but on the whole unlikely, that the story of the oath is a Norman invention. But there is a third explanation, the one which the English artists of the Bayeux Tapestry may secretly be trying to give us: Harold falls into William's hands by mischance, is forced to swear the oath, and returns shamefacedly to a horrified King Edward. Whichever version is true (and on balance the Norman one may have the best claim after all), many contemporaries believed that William had right on his side as well as might.

The events of the last two years moved quickly. During 1065 Northumbria rebelled against Earl Tostig. Harold mediated, but the local nominee was upheld: Tostig went into exile, henceforth his brother's enemy. On 5 January 1066 King Edward died. Urgent military need overrode legality, and the Witan elected Harold as king. This was the signal for his two adult rivals. Harold Hardrada of Norway was the first to move: aided by the exiled Tostig, he invaded Northumbria during the summer and occupied York. Harold, who was awaiting the expected invasion from Normandy, was forced to move north. At Stamford Bridge near York he met and defeated the Norwegian forces on 25 September. Hardrada and Tostig were both killed, and King Harold recovered Northumbria.

Meanwhile Duke William's fleet, which had been delayed by bad weather, landed at Pevensey on 28 September. Harold rushed southwards; but the preparations which he had made two months earlier had fallen apart, and the core of his army was exhausted. On 14 October 1066, the English and Norman armies met near Hastings. Harold's forces gathered on the crest of a hill and formed a wall of shields. The battle lasted all day, and at first the English position seemed strong. Apparently it was lost through lack of discipline rather than lack of force. Sections of Harold's army seem to have been enticed down the slope in pursuit of real or feigned retreats, and then cut off and overwhelmed. Gradually the English troops were broken up; the centre held until dusk, but the outcome was already clear when Harold fell on the spot marked in later centuries by the high altar of Battle Abbey.

William advanced to Dover and then to Canterbury, where he received the submission of Winchester. But his main objective was London, for there the core of the English resistance had gathered under Edgar Atheling. Meeting opposition at London Bridge, William encircled the city leaving a trail of devastation. Meanwhile the Atheling's party was crumbling, and when William reached Berkhamsted the English nobles, headed by Edgar himself, met him and offered their fealty. Alfred's family had survived Danes, Norsemen, and Danes again, but at last a foreign dynasty had supplanted it for good.

FURTHER READING

1. ROMAN BRITAIN

BEFORE THE ROMAN CONQUEST

Richard Bradley, *The Prehistoric Settlement of Britain* (London, 1978), particularly readable.

Barry Cunliffe, *Iron Age Communities in Britain* (2nd edn. London, 1978), general account of the centuries immediately before the Roman Conquest.

John Brailsford, *Early Celtic Masterpieces from Britain in the British Museum* (London, 1975).

GENERAL SURVEYS

Sheppard Frere, *Britannia: a History of Roman Britain* (3rd edn. London, 1987), a standard work.

Peter Salway, *Roman Britain* (*Oxford History of England*, vol. 1a) (Oxford, 1981), large-scale general history, with essays on major themes.

Malcolm Todd, *Roman Britain 55 BC–AD 400: the Province beyond Ocean* (*Fontana History of England*) (London, 1981), perceptive and up-to-date narrative.

John Wacher, *Roman Britain* (London, 1978).

Peter A. Clayton (ed.), *A Companion to Roman Britain* (Oxford, 1980), exceptionally well-illustrated essays.

Roger J. A. Wilson, *A Guide to the Roman Remains in Britain* (2nd edn. London, 1980), recommended to those wishing to visit the accessible material remains of the period.

Ordnance Survey, *Map of Roman Britain* (4th edn. Southampton, 1978), 2 sheets, scale 1 : 625,000, and gazetteer.

Philip Dixon, *Barbarian Europe* (*The Making of the Past*) (Oxford, 1976), excellent, well-illustrated background reading, helping to place the end of Roman Britain in its European context.

SPECIAL ASPECTS

Anthony Birley, *The People of Roman Britain* (London, 1979), illuminating study based on the people known by name in Roman Britain.

A. L. F. Rivet and Colin Smith, *The Place-Names of Roman Britain* (London, 1979), major work of reference: gazetteer, accompanied by linguistic and geographical analysis.

P. A. Holder, *The Roman Army in Britain* (London, 1982), welcome first modern account.

David J. Breeze, *The Northern Frontiers of Roman Britain* (London, 1982), current thought, well-presented.

Ralph Merrifield, *London: City of the Romans* (London, 1983).

J. M. C. Toynbee, *Art in Britain under the Romans* (Oxford, 1964), enormously learned, wide-ranging, and clear.

Charles Thomas, *Christianity in Britain to AD 500* (London, 1981), thought-provoking re-examination.

Ralph Merrifield, *The Archaeology of Ritual and Magic* (London, 1987), includes much illuminating reinterpretation of Romano-British material.

2.   THE ANGLO-SAXON PERIOD

GENERAL HISTORY

F. M. Stenton, *Anglo-Saxon England* (3rd edn. Oxford, 1971), the standard history.

J. Campbell (ed.), *The Anglo-Saxons* (Oxford, 1982), an outstandingly good recent book, with many new ideas and splendid illustrations.

P. Hunter Blair, *An introduction to Anglo-Saxon England* (Cambridge, 1956), summarizes the main events and themes.

ORIGINAL SOURCES

The Anglo-Saxon Chronicle, trans. G. N. Garmonsway (London, 1953); the late Anglo-Saxon vernacular chronicle, providing contemporary comment from Alfred's reign onwards.

Bede, *Ecclesiastical History of the English People*, trans. L. Sherley-Price (rev. edn. Harmondsworth, 1968), a brilliant and vivid narrative account written in the early eighth century, the most important single source for earlier Anglo-Saxon history.

ARCHAEOLOGY, ART, AND LITERATURE

R. L. Bruce-Mitford, *The Sutton Hoo Ship Burial: a Handbook* (3rd edn. London, 1979), a well-illustrated account of the most important archaeological discovery from the Anglo-Saxon period.

The Earliest English Poems, trans. M. Alexander (2nd edn. Harmonds-worth, 1977), translations of the more important Anglo-Saxon poems, including *The Battle of Maldon* and selections from *Beowulf*.

H. M. and Joan Taylor, *Anglo-Saxon Architecture*, i–iii (Cambridge, 1965–78), a comprehensive account of the surviving Anglo-Saxon churches.

D. Talbot Rice, *English Art 871–1100* (Oxford, 1952), a well-illustrated general account.

D. M. Wilson (ed.), *The archaeology of Anglo-Saxon England* (Cambridge, 1976), chapters by several authors on the various kinds of physical evidence for the period.

THE MERCIAN SUPREMACY

A. Dornier (ed.), *Mercian Studies* (Leicester, 1977), a collection of essays relating to the Mercian region, especially during the eighth century.

LATE ANGLO-SAXON KINGSHIP AND GOVERNMENT

F. Barlow, *Edward the Confessor* (London, 1970), the standard bio-graphy.

D. Hill (ed.), *Ethelred the Unready: papers from the Millenary Confer-ence* (Oxford, 1978), a recent collection of important and original studies on the late tenth and early eleventh centuries.

THE CHURCH

H. Mayr-Harting, *The coming of Christianity to Anglo-Saxon England* (London, 1972), the best general account of the conversions.

P. Hunter Blair, *The world of Bede* (London, 1970), religion and learning in eighth-century Northumbria.

M. Deanesly, *The pre-Conquest church in England* (London, 1961), a general survey of ecclesiastical institutions.

SCOTLAND AND WALES: GENERAL HISTORY

A. A. M. Duncan, *Scotland: the making of the kingdom* (Edinburgh, 1975).

W. Davies, *Wales in the early Middle Ages* (Leicester, 1982).

CHRONOLOGY

VOL. I. ROMAN AND ANGLO-SAXON BRITAIN

55–54 BC	Expeditions of Caesar
49 BC	*Caesar defeats Pompey: effective end of Roman Republic**
	Julio-Claudian Emperors (27 BC–AD 68
34–26 BC	Projected expeditions of Augustus
	Britain between the invasions: period of political and economic change
by 12 BC	*Permanent Roman bases on Rhine*
AD 40	Expedition of Gaius cancelled
	Claudius (41–54)
by 43	Death of Cunobelinus
43	Claudian invasion
by 47	Conquest of south and east of England completed
49	Foundation of Colchester
c.50	Foundation of London
51	Defeat and capture of Caratacus
	Nero (54–68)
61	Revolt of Boudica
68–9	*'Year of the Four Emperors'*
	Flavian Emperors (69–96)
70–84	Conquest of Wales and north completed
	Conquest of Scotland
	Trajan (98–117)
c.100	Scotland temporarily lost: frontier on Tyne–Solway line *Hadrian (117–38)*
122	Hadrian in Britain: the Wall begun
	Antonine Emperors (138–92)
	Antoninus Pius (138–61)
140–3	Antonine advance into Scotland: by 143 Antonine Wall begun
c.158	Serious trouble in the north
? c.160	Temporary reoccupation of Antonine Wall

* Entries in *italics* denote events belonging to the history of the Roman Empire.

	Marcus Aurelius (161–80); major wars on the Danube
? c.163	Hadrian's Wall restored
193	Clodius Albinus proclaimed in Britain
	Severan Emperors (193–235)
196–213	Britain becomes two provinces
208–11	Campaigns of Septimius Severus and Caracalla in Scotland
235–70	*Imperial crisis: civil wars and invasions in East and West*
260–73	*'Gallic Empire'*
270s	Renewed growth in Britain
	Diocletian (284–305)
	'The Tetarchy'
287–96	Carausius and Allectus
296	Britain recovered by Constantius
after 296	Britain becomes a civil diocese of four provinces
	House of Constantius (305–63)
306	Campaign of Constantius I in Scotland; Constantine the Great proclaimed at York
324	*Constantine sole emperor; foundation of Constantinople*
340–69	Period of severe stress: internal troubles, harassment by barbarians
350	*Magnentius proclaimed in Gaul*
353	*Constantius II sole emperor*
353	Purge by Paul the Chain
	House of Valentinian (364–92)
367–9	'Barbarian Conspiracy', recovery and restoration of Britain by the elder Theodosius
	House of Theodosius (379–455)
	Theodosius the Great (379–95)
383	Magnus Maximus proclaimed in Britain; victory over Picts
	Honorius (395–423)
398–400	Victories over Picts, Scots, Saxons
400–2	Possible troop withdrawals by Stilicho
402/3	*Western imperial court withdrawn from Milan to Ravenna*
406	Britain revolts from Honorius: two emperors proclaimed

407	Constantine III proclaimed in Britain
	Constantine III rules from Arles (407–11)
409	Britain revolts from Constantine III: end of Roman rule in Britain
410	'Rescript of Honorius': letter to Britons (?), significance disputed
429	St. Germanus visits Britain
c.450	The *adventus Saxonum*: Hengest and Horsa settle in Kent (traditional date)
455	Hengest rebels against Vortigern (traditional date)
477	Saxon settlement of Sussex (traditional date)
495	Saxon settlement of Wessex (traditional date)
c.500	Battle of *Mons Badonicus*
560	Æthelberht, later over-king, becomes king in Kent
577	The West Saxons capture Gloucester, Cirencester and Bath
597	St. Augustine's mission arrives in Kent
616	Raedwald of East Anglia, as over-king, makes Edwin king of Northumbria
c.624	Death of Raedwald, and his probable burial in the Sutton Hoo barrow
627	Conversion of Edwin and the Northumbrian court
633	Battle of Heavenfield; Oswald of Northumbria becomes over-king
635	Conversion of King Cynegils of Wessex
642	Oswald is killed at Oswestry by King Penda of Mercia
655	Penda is defeated and killed at the *Winwaed* by Oswy of Northumbria, who becomes over-king
664	Synod of Whitby
669	Arrival of Archbishop Theodore
672	Synod of Hertford; battle of the Trent, marking the beginnings of the rise of Mercia
685–8	Expansion of Wessex under Caedwalla to include Kent, Surrey and Sussex
716	Æthelbald become king of Mercia
731	Bede completes his *Ecclesiastical History*
746–7	First Council of Clofesho
757	Death of Æthelbald; Offa becomes king of Mercia
786	Legatine Council held under Offa

793–5	Danish raids on Lindisfarne, Jarrow, and Iona
796	Death of Offa
825	Egbert of Wessex defeats Mercia and annexes Kent, Essex, Surrey, and Sussex
835	Big Danish raid on Kent
865	The Danish 'Great Army' lands
867	Northumbria falls to the Danes
870	East Anglia falls to the Danes; murder of St. Edmund
871	The Danes attack Wessex; Alfred becomes king
874	Mercia falls to the Danes
878	(March) The Danes drive Alfred into the Somerset marshes
	(May) Alfred defeats the Danes at Edington; Guthrum is baptized
899	Death of Alfred; Edward 'the Elder' becomes king of Wessex
910–20	Edward and Æthelflaed reconquer most of the Danelaw
919	Norse kingdom of York is founded by Raegnald
924	Death of Edward; Athelstan becomes king
937	Athelstan defeats the Norse, Scots and Strathclyde Welsh at Brunanburh
939	Death of Athelstan; Edmund become king
940	Dunstan begin to refound Glastonbury as a regular monastic house
946	Death of Edmund
954	The last king of York is deposed
959	Edgar becomes king
960	Dunstan becomes Archbishop of Canterbury
c.970	*Regularis Concordia* is compiled
973	Edgar is crowned and consecrated, and receives the submission of British princes
975	Death of Edgar; Edward 'the Martyr' becomes king
979	Murder of Edward; Æthelred 'the Unready' becomes king
991	The Danes defeat Alderman Byrhtnoth and the Essex levies at Maldon; treaty between England and Normandy
1002	Æthelred orders the massacre of all Danes in England

1003	Danish invasion led by King Swein
1013	Swein returns with a new army; the Danelaw accepts him as king
1014	Swein dies; the Danish army in England elect Cnut as their king
1016	(April) Æthelred dies; Edmund 'Ironside' becomes king (autumn) Cnut defeats Edmund at Ashingdon; Edmund dies and Cnut becomes King of all England
1017	Cnut divides England into four earldoms
1035	Death of Cnut
1037	Harold becomes king
1040	Death of Harold; Harthacnut becomes king
1042	Death of Harthacnut; Edward 'the Confessor' becomes king
1051–2	Conflict between King Edward and Godwin earl of Wessex
1053	Death of Godwin; his son Harold becomes earl of Wessex
1064–5	Earl Harold visits Duke William in Normandy
1066	(January) Death of King Edward; Earl Harold becomes king
	(September) King Harold of England defeats and kills King Harold of Norway at Stamford Bridge
	(October) Duke William of Normandy defeats and kills King Harold of England at Hastings

VOL. 2 THE MIDDLE AGES

1066	(December) William is consecrated king
1067–70	English rebellions
1069–70	The harrying of the north
1086	Domesday Survey carried out
1087	Death of William I; accession of William II Rufus
1088	Rebellion in support of Robert Curthose
1093	Anselm appointed Archbishop of Canterbury
1096	Robert pawns Normandy ot Rufus
1100	Death of William Rufus; accession of Henry I
1101	Invasion of Robert Curthose
1106	Battle of Tinchebray; Curthose imprisoned; Henry I takes Normandy
1107	Settlement of Investiture Dispute in England

1120	Wreck of the White Ship
1128	Marriage of Empress Matilda to Geoffrey of Anjou
1135	Death of Henry I; accession of Stephen
1139–53	Civil war in England
1141	Battle of Lincoln; Stephen captured; later exchanged for Robert of Gloucester
1141–5	Geoffrey of Anjou conquers Normandy
1149	Cession of Northumbria to David of Scotland
1152	Henry of Anjou (later Henry II) marries Eleanor of Aquitaine
1153	Henry invades England; he and Stephen come to terms
1154	Death of Stephen; accession of Henry II
1157	Henry regains Northumbria
1162	Becket appointed Archbishop of Canterbury
1164	Council and Constitutions of Clarendon; Becket goes into exile
1166	Assize of Clarendon
1169–72	English conquest of Ireland begins
1170	Coronation of the young king; murder of Becket
1173–4	Rebellion against Henry II; William 'the Lion' (king of Scotland) invades the north
1183	Death of the young king
1189	Death of Henry II; accession of Richard I
1190–92	Richard I on crusade
1193–4	Richard in prison in Germany
1193–1205	Hubert Walter, Archbishop of Canterbury (justiciar 1194–8; chancellor 1199–1205)
1197	Death of Rhys of Deheubarth
1199	Death of Richard I; accession of John; establishment of Chancery Rolls
1203–4	Philip Augustus conquers Anjou and Normandy
1208–14	Interdict in England
1214	Battle of Bouvines: French victory
1215	Magna Carta; civil war in England
1216	Louis (later Louis VIII) invades; death of John; accession of Henry III
1217	Battles of Lincoln and Dover; Louis withdraws
1221–4	Arrival of Dominican and Franciscan Friars in England
1224	Louis VIII completes conquest of Poitou

1232	Dismissal of Hubert de Burgh
1240	Death of Llywelyn the Great
1254	Henry III accepts papal offer of throne of Sicily
1258	Barons take over royal government; provisions of Oxford
1259	Treaty of Paris between England and France
1264	Battle of Lewes; Henry III captured; government of Simon de Montfort
1265	Battle of Evesham; killing of Simon de Montfort
1267	Henry recognizes Llywelyn ap Gruffydd as Prince of Wales
1272	Death of Henry III; accession of Edward I
1276–7	First Welsh War
1282–3	Edward's conquest of Wales
1286–9	Edward I in Gascony
1291	Edward I asserts his overlordship over Scotland
1294	War with France begins
1295	Franco-Scottish alliance
1296	Edward I invades Scotland; his conflict with the Church
1297	Edward I's conflict with his magnates; his expedition to Flanders
1306	Rebellion of Robert Bruce
1307	Death of Edward I; accession of Edward II
1314	Scottish victory at Bannockburn
1315–16	Great famine
1321–2	Civil war in England
1327	Deposition and death of Edward II; accession of Edward III
1330	Edward III takes the reins of government
1337	The Hundred Years War begins
1339–41	Political crisis in England
1346	English victories at Crécy and Neville's Cross
1347	English capture Calais
1348	First occurrence of plague in England
1356	English victory at Poitiers
1361	Second major occurrence of plague
1376	'Good Parliament' meets; death of Edward, the Black Prince
1377	Death of Edward III; accession of Richard II

1381	The Peasants' Revolt
1382	Condemnation of John Wycliffe's works
1388	'Merciless Parliament' meets; battle of Otterburn against the Scots
1389	Richard II declares himself of age
1394–5	Richard II's expedition to Ireland
1396	Anglo-French treaty
1397–9	Richard II's 'tyranny'
1399	Deposition of Richard II; accession of Henry IV
1400	Rebellion of Owain Glyndŵr begins (to 1410)
1403	Henry Hotspur defeated at Shrewsbury
1405	Execution of Archbishop Scrope of York
1408	Defeat of the earl of Northumberland at Bramham Moor
1413	Death of Henry IV; accession of Henry V
1415	English victory at Agincourt
1419–20	English conquest of Normandy
1420	Anglo-French treaty of Troyes
1422	Death of Henry V; accession of Henry VI
1435	Death of John, duke of Bedford; Franco-Burgundian treaty of Arras
1436–7	Henry VI comes of age
1445	Henry VI marries Margaret of Anjou
1449–50	French overrun Normandy
1450	Murder of the duke of Suffolk; John Cade's rebellion
1453	French overrun Gascony; Henry VI becomes ill
1455	Battle of St. Albans between Richard, duke of York and the royalist forces
1459	Defeat of the duke of York at Blore Heath and Ludford Bridge
1461	Deposition of Henry VI; accession of Edward IV
1465	Capture of Henry VI
1469	Rebellion of Richard, earl of Warwick and George, duke of Clarence
1470	Deposition of Edward IV; return of Henry VI
1471	Return of Edward IV; death of the earl of Warwick at Barnet; death of Henry VI
1475	Edward IV's expedition to France; Anglo-French treaty of Picquigny

1558	New Book of Rates; accession of Elizabeth I
1559	Peace of Cateau-Cambrésis; religious Settlement in England
1566	Archbishop Parker's *Advertisements* demand religious conformity
1568	Mary Stuart flees to England
1569	Northern Rebellion
1570	Papal bull declares Elizabeth excommunicated and deposed
1580	Jesuit missionaries arrive in England
1585	War with Spain
1587	Execution of Mary Stuart
1588	Defeat of the Spanish Armada
1594	Bad harvests begin
1601	Essex's rebellion
1603	Death of Elizabeth; accession of James VI of Scotland as James I; peace in Ireland; Millenary Petition of the Puritans
1604	Peace with Spain (treaty of London); Hampton Court Conference (king, bishops, Puritans)
1605	Gunpowder Plot, the last major Catholic conspiracy
1606–7	Failure of James's plans for union of kingdoms
1607	Settlement of Virginia
1609	Rebellion of the Northern Earls in Ireland; beginnings of the Planting of Ulster by Scots and English Protestants
1610	Failure of Great Contract (reform of royal finance)
1611	Publication of Authorized Version of the Bible (Anglican–Puritan co-operation)
1612	Death of Prince Henry, James's promising elder son
1613	Marriage of Princess Elizabeth to Elector Palatine, Protestant zealot, enmeshed Britain in continental politics
1617–29	Ascendancy of George Villiers, duke of Buckingham
1919–22	Inigo Jones designs the Banqueting House, the first major royal public building since the reign of Henry VIII
1620	Pilgrim Fathers inaugurate religious migration to New England

1622–3	Prince Charles and Buckingham go to Spain to woo the king's daughter and are rebuffed
1624–30	War with Spain
1625	Death of James I; accession of Charles I and marriage to Henrietta Maria, sister of Louis XIII of France
1626–9	War with France
1628	Petition of Right; publication of Harvey's work on the circulation of the blood; assassination of Buckingham
1629	Charles I dissolves Parliament, determines to govern without one
1630	Large-scale emigration to Massachusetts begins
1633	William Laud translated to be Archbishop of Canterbury
1634–40	Ship Money case
1637	Hampden's case supports Charles I's claim to collect Ship Money
1637–40	Breakdown of Charles's government of Scotland and two attempts to impose his will by force
1640	Long Parliament summoned
1641	Remodelling of government in England and Scotland; abolition of conciliar courts, abolition of prerogative taxation, triennial bill, Grand Remonstrance; rebellion of Ulster Catholics
1642	King's attempt on the Five Members; his withdrawal from London; the 19 Propositions; the resort of arms: Civil War
1643	King's armies prosper; Scots invade on side of Parliament
1644	Parliamentary armies prosper, especially in the decisive battle of the war, Marston Moor (June)
1645	'Clubmen' risings of armed neutrals threaten both sides; Royalist armies disintegrate, but parliamentary forces reorganized (New Model Army)
1646	King surrenders to the Scots; bishops and Book of Common Prayer abolished, Presbyterian Church established
1647	Army revolt; radical movements criticize parliamentary tyranny; king prevaricates

1648	Second Civil War: Scots now side with the king and are defeated; provincial risings (Kent, Colchester, South Wales, Yorks., etc.) crushed
1649	Trial and execution of Charles I: England a Republic
1649–53	Government by sovereign single-chamber assembly, the 'Rump' Parliament thoroughly purged of royalists and moderates
1649–50	Oliver Cromwell conquers Ireland (Drogheda massacre)
1650–2	Oliver Cromwell conquers Scotland (battles of Dunbar and Worcester)
1651	Thomas Hobbes's *Leviathan* published
1652–4	First Dutch War
1653	Cromwell dissolves Rump, creates the Nominated or Barebones Assembly; it surrenders power back to him, and he becomes Lord Protector under a paper constitution (*The Instrument of Government*)
1655–60	War with Spain
1655	Royalist insurrection (Penruddock's rising) is a complete failure
1657	*Instrument of Government* replaced by a parliamentary paper constitution, the *Humble Petition and Advice*; Cromwell rejects title of King and remains Lord Protector, but nominates his own House of Lords
1658	Cromwell dies and is succeeded by his son Richard
1659	Richard overthrown by the army; Rump restored but displeases many in the army
1660	Charles II restored
1662	Church of England restored; Royal Society receives its Charter
1663	Failure of first royal attempt to grant religious toleration
1665–7	Second Dutch War
1665	Great Plague (final major outbreak)
1666	Great Fire of London
1667	Milton's *Paradise Lost* published
1672–3	Failure of second royal attempt to grant religious toleration
1672–4	Third Dutch War

1714	Death of Anne; accession of George I
1715	Jacobite rebellion aimed at overthrowing the Hanoverian succession fails
1716	Septennial Act sets the maximum duration of a parliament at seven years
1717	Whig split; suspension of convocation
1720	South Sea Bubble: many investors ruined after speculation in the stock of the South Sea Company
1721	Walpole ministry
1722	Atterbury Plot, the most notable Jacobite plot
1726	Jonathan Swift's *Gulliver's Travels* published
1727	Death of George I; accession of George II
1729	Alexander Pope's *Dunciad* published
1730	Walpole/Townshend split
1733	Excise crisis: Walpole has to abandon his plans to reorganize the customs and excise
1737	Death of Queen Caroline
1738	Wesley's 'conversion': the start of Methodism
1739	War of Jenkins' Ear: Anglo-Spanish naval war
1740	War of the Austrian Succession
1741	Samuel Richardson's *Pamela* published
1742	Fall of Walpole
1744	Ministry of Pelham
1745	Jacobite Rebellion led by 'Bonnie Prince Charlie'
1746	Battle of Culloden: the duke of Cumberland routs the Jacobite army
1748	Peace of Aix-la-Chapelle concludes War of the Austrian Succession
1752	Adoption of Gregorian Calendar
1753	Jewish Naturalization Bill
1754	Newcastle ministry
1756	Seven Years War: Britain allied with Frederick the Great of Prussian against France, Austria, and Russia
1757	Pitt–Newcastle ministry; battle of Plassey: British victory over Bengal
1759	Capture of Quebec: British victory over the French
1760	Death of George II; accession of George III
1761	Laurence Sterne's *Tristram Shandy* published
1762	Bute's ministry
1763	Peace of Paris concludes Seven Years War; Grenville

	ministry; Wilkes and General Warrants
1765	Rockingham ministry; American Stamp Act attempts to make the defence of the American colonies self-financing: repealed 1766
1766	Chatham ministry
1768	Grafton ministry; Middlesex election crisis
1769	James Watt's steam engine patented
1770	Lord North's ministry; Edmund Burke's *Thoughts on the Present Discontents* published; Falkland Islands crisis
1773	Boston Tea Party: American colonists protest against the East India Company's monopoly of tea exports to America
1774	Coercive Acts passed in retaliation for Boston Tea Party
1776	Declaration of American Independence; Edward Gibbon's *Decline and Fall* and Adam Smith's *Wealth of Nations* published
1779	Wyvill's Association movement
1780	Gordon Riots develop from a procession to petition parliament against the Catholic Relief Act
1781	Surrender at Yorktown: American victory over British troops
1782	Second Rockingham ministry
1783	Shelburne ministry; Peace of Versailles recognizes independence of American colonies; Fox–North coalition; Younger Pitt's ministry
1784	East India Act
1785	Pitt's motion for parliamentary reform defeated
1786	Eden commercial treaty with France
1789	French Revolution
1790	Edmund Burke's *Reflections on the Revolution in France* published
1791	Thomas Paine's *The Rights of Man* published
1792	Coal gas used for lighting; Mary Wollstonecraft's *Vindication of the Rights of Women* published
1793	Outbreak of war with France; voluntary Board of Agriculture set up; commercial depression
1795	'Speenhamland' system of outdoor relief adopted, making up wages to equal cost of subsistence

1796	Vaccination against smallpox introduced
1798	T. R. Malthus's *Essay on Population* published; tax of ten per cent on incomes over £200 introduced
1799	Trade Unions suppressed; Napoleon appointed First Consul in France
1799–1801	Commercial boom
1801	Union with Ireland; first British Census
1802	Peace with France; Peel introduces first factory legislation
1803	War with France; General Enclosure Act simplifies process of enclosure of common land
1805	Battle of Trafalgar: Nelson defeats the French and Spanish fleets
1809–10	Commercial boom
1811	Depression because of Orders in Council; 'Luddite' disturbances in Nottinghamshire and Yorkshire; George, Prince of Wales, made Prince Regent
1813	East India Company's monopoly abolished
1815	Battle of Waterloo: defeat of Napoleon; peace in Europe: Congress of Vienna; Corn Law passed setting price of corn at 80s. per quarter
1815–17	Commercial boom
1817	Slump; the Blanketeers' march and other disturbances
1819	Peterloo massacre: troops intervene at mass reform meeting, killing 11 and wounding 400
1820	Death of George III; accession of George IV
1821–3	Famine in Ireland
1824	Commercial boom
1825	Trade Unions legalized; Stockton and Darlington railway opens; commercial depression
1829	Catholic Emancipation, ending most denials or restrictions of Catholic civil rights, ownership of property, and holding of public office
1830	Death of George IV; accession of William IV; Liverpool and Manchester railway opens
1830–2	First major cholera epidemic; Whigs in power under Grey
1831	'Swing' riots in rural areas against the mechanization of agriculture
1832	Great Reform Bill brings climax to period of political

	reform, enlarging the franchise and restructuring representation in Parliament
1833	Factory Act limits child labour; beginning of Oxford Movement in Anglican Church
1834	Slavery abolished in the British Empire; parish workhouses instituted; Robert Owen founds the Grand National Consolidated Trade Union: action by government against 'illegal oaths' in unionism results in failure of GNCTU and transportation of six 'Tolpuddle Martyrs'
1835	Municipal Reform Act extends local government franchise to all ratepayers
1835–6	Commercial boom: 'little' railway mania
1837	Death of William IV; accession of Queen Victoria
1838	Anti-Corn Law League established; People's Charter drafted
1839	Chartist riots
1840	Penny post instituted
1841	Tories in power: Peel ministry
1844	Bank Charter Act; Rochdale Co-operative Society founded; Royal Commission on Health of Towns
1844–5	Railway mania: massive speculation and investment leads to building of 5,000 miles of track; potato famine begins in Ireland
1846	Corn Law abolished; Whigs in power
1848	Revolutions in Europe; Public Health Act

VOL. 5 THE MODERN AGE

1851	Great Exhibition
1852	Derby's first minority Conservative government
1852–5	Aberdeen's coalition government
1853	Gladstone's first budget
1854	Northcote–Trevelyan civil service report
1854–6	Crimean War, defending European interests in the Middle East against Russia
1855	Palmerston's first government
1857–8	Second Opium War opens China to European trade
1858–9	Derby's second minority Conservative government
1858	Indian Mutiny and India Act
1859	Publication of Darwin's *Origin of Species*

1859-65	Palmerston's second Liberal government
1860	Anglo-French 'Cobden' treaty and Gladstone's budget codify and extend principles of free trade
1861	Death of Albert, Prince Consort
1862	Limited Liability Act provides vital stimulus to accumulation of capital in shares
1865	Death of Palmerston (October)
1865-6	Russell's second Liberal government
1866	Russell–Gladstone moderate Reform Bill fails
1866-8	Derby's third minority Conservative government
1867	Derby–Disraeli Reform Act; Dominion of Canada Act
1868	Disraeli succeeds Derby as Prime Minister (February)
1868-74	Gladstone's first Liberal government
1869	Suez Canal opened; Irish Church disestablished
1870	Irish Land Act; Forster–Ripon English Elementary Education Act; Married Women's Property Act extends the rights of women in marriage
1872	Scottish Education Act
1873	Gladstone government resigns after defeat on Irish Universities Bill; Disraeli declines to take office
1874-80	Disraeli's second Conservative government
1875	Disraeli buys Suez Canal shares, gaining a controlling interest for Britain
1875	Agricultural depression deepens
1875-6	R. A. Cross's Conservative social reforms passed
1876	Victoria proclaimed Empress of India; massacres of Christians in Turkish Bulgaria provoke anti-Turkish campaign in Britain, led by Gladstone
1877	Confederation of British and Boer states in South Africa
1878	Congress of Berlin; Disraeli announces 'peace with honour'
1879	Trade depression; Zulu War: British defeated at Isandhlwana, win at Ulundi
1879-80	Gladstone's Midlothian campaign denounces imperialism in Afghanistan and South Africa
1880-5	Gladstone's second Liberal government
1880-1	First Anglo-Boer War
1881	Irish Land and Coercion Acts

1882	Britain occupies Egypt; Triple Alliance between Germany, Austria, and Italy
1884–5	Reform and Redistribution Acts
1885	Death of Gordon at Khartoum; Burma annexed; Salisbury's first (minority) Conservative government
1886	Royal Niger Company chartered; gold found in Transvaal; Gladstone's third Liberal government introduces first Home Rule Bill for Ireland: Liberal Party splits
1886–92	Salisbury's second (Conservative–Liberal-Unionist) government
1887	British East Africa Company chartered
1888	County Councils Act establishes representative county authorities
1889	London dock strike; British South Africa Company chartered
1892–4	Gladstone's fourth (minority) Liberal government
1893	Second Home Rule Bill rejected by the Lords; Independent Labour Party founded
1894–5	Rosebery's minority Liberal government
1895–1902	Salisbury's third Unionist ministry
1896–8	Sudan conquered
1898	German naval expansion begins
1899–1902	Second Anglo-Boer War
1899	(autumn)British disasters in South Africa
1900	Khaki election won by Salisbury; formation of Labour Representation Committee; Commonwealth of Australia Act
1901	Death of Victoria; accession of Edward VII
1902	Balfour's Education Act; Anglo-Japanese alliance
1902–5	Balfour's Unionist government
1903	Chamberlain's Tariff Reform campaign starts
1904	Anglo-French *Entente*
1905–8	Campbell-Bannerman's Liberal government
1906	Liberals win general election (January); Labour Party formed
1907	Anglo-Russian *Entente*
1908–15	Asquith's Liberal government
1908	Asquith's Old Age Pensions plan introduced

1909	Churchill's Employment Exchanges introduced; Lloyd George's budget rejected by Lords; Union of South Africa Act
1910	(January) General election: Liberal government retains office
	(May) Death of Edward VII; accession of George V
	(December) General election: Liberal government again retains office
1911	Parliament Act curtails power of the House of Lords, establishes five-yearly elections; Lloyd George's National Insurance Act; Moroccan crisis
1911–12	Railway, mining, and coal strikes
1912	Anglo-German navy talks fail
1912–14	Third Home Rule Act (for Ireland) and Welsh Church Disestablishment Act passed, but suspended
1914	(28 June) Assassination of Archduke Ferdinand at Sarajevo
	(4 August) British Empire enters the First World War
1915–16	Dardanelles expedition, ending in British withdrawal from Gallipoli
1916	Battle of the Somme; battle of Jutland; Lloyd George succeeds Asquith as Prime Minister
1917	Battle of Passchendaele
1918	End of First World War (11 November); Lloyd George coalition government returned in 'coupon election' (December)
1919	Treaty of Versailles establishes peace in Europe
1921	Miners seek support of dockers' and railwaymen's unions (the 'Triple Alliance') in major strike: on 'Black Friday' the dockers and railwaymen back down, and the alliance is broken; Lloyd George concludes treaty with Sinn Fein
1922	Fall of Lloyd George; Bonar Law heads Conservative government
1923	Baldwin becomes Conservative Prime Minister; general election
1924	(January) MacDonald leads first Labour government
	(November) Conservatives return to office under Baldwin

1925	Britain goes back on the gold standard
1926	General Strike (3–12 May)
1929	General election; MacDonald leads second Labour government
1931	Financial crisis and run on the pound; Britain abandons the gold standard; MacDonald resigns and is returned in the election to head National government
1932	Ottawa Conference on imperial trade institutes protective tarriffs
1935	Conservatives win general election: Baldwin succeeds MacDonald as Prime Minister; Hoare–Laval pact on Abyssinia; Government of India Act
1936	Death of King George V; abdication of Edward VIII: George VI becomes king
1937	Neville Chamberlain succeeds Baldwin as Conservative Prime Minister
1938	Chamberlain meets Hitler at Berchtesgaden, Godesberg, and Munich
1939	British guarantee to Poland; British Empire declares war on Germany (3 September)
1940	Churchill succeeds Chamberlain as Prime Minister; withdrawal from Dunkirk; Battle of Britain
1941	*Luftwaffe* 'blitz' on many British cities; Soviet Union and United States enter the war
1942	Loss of Singapore; Montgomery's victory at El Alamein; battle of Stalingrad; Beveridge Report on social security
1943	Successful campaign in North Africa; Anglo-American armies invade Italy
1944	D-day invasion of France; Butler's Education Act
1945	End of war in Europe (8 May) and in far East (15 August); general election: massive Labour victory and Attlee becomes Prime Minister
1947	Coal and other industries nationalized; convertibility crisis; transfer of power to independent India, Pakistan, and Burma
1949	NATO founded; devaluation of the pound by Cripps
1950	General election: Labour retains power by narrow

	majority; outbreak of war in Korea
1951	Festival of Britain; general election: Conservatives defeat Labour, and Churchill again becomes Prime Minister
1952	Death of King George VI; Queen Elizabeth II proclaimed
1954	British troops withdraw from Egypt
1955	Eden becomes Prime Minister; general election won by Conservatives
1956	Anglo-French invasion of Suez, followed by withdrawal
1957	Eden resigns; Macmillan becomes Prime Minister
1959	General election: Conservatives win with larger majority
1963	French veto Britain's application to join the European Common Market; test-ban treaty in Moscow limits nuclear testing; Douglas-Home succeeds Macmillan as Prime Minister
1964	General election: Labour under Harold Wilson win narrow majority
1966	General election: Labour win with much larger majority
1967	Devaluation of the pound
1970	General election: Conservatives under Edward Heath returned to office
1972	National miners' strike; Stormont government abolished in Northern Ireland
1973	Britain enters European Common Market
1974	National miners' strike; two general elections: Labour under Harold Wilson win both with narrow majorities
1975	Popular referendum confirms British membership of the Common Market
1976	Economic crisis: Britain obtains help from International Monetary Fund
1979	Devolution referendums in Wales and Scotland; general election: Conservatives under Mrs Thatcher returned to office; independence granted to Zimbabwe (Rhodesia)
1980	Britain becomes self-sufficient in North Sea oil

1981	Social Democratic Party founded
1982	Britain defeats Argentina in war over the Falkland Islands
1983	General election: Mrs Thatcher's Conservative government returned with massive majority; Cruise missiles installed
1984	Miners' strike
1985	Miners' strike ends after a year; Anglo-Irish Hillsborough Agreement signed
1986	Channel Tunnel treaty signed; 'Big Bang' in Stock Exchange
1987	General election: Mrs Thatcher's Conservative government again returned with a majority of over 100; Stock Exchange collapse in the autumn

THE HOUSE OF WESSEX
802–1066

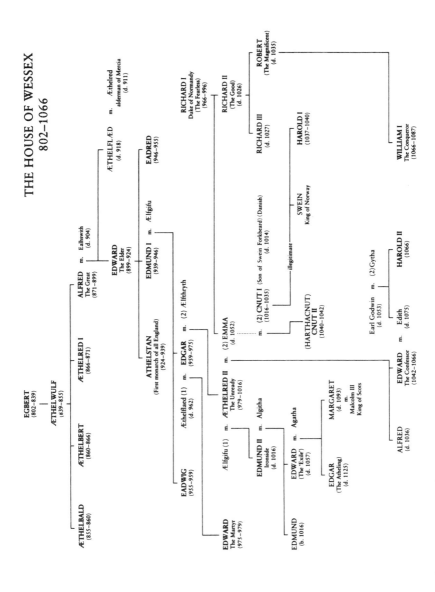